FRAGILE X
FRAGILE HOPE

FRAGILE X
FRAGILE HOPE

Finding Joy in Parenting a Child with Special Needs

ELIZABETH GRIFFIN

P.O. Box 635, Lynnwood, WA 98046

Emerald Books are distributed through YWAM Publishing. For a full list of titles, visit www.ywampublishing.com or call 1-800-922-2143.

We can do no great things,
only small things with great love.
—MOTHER TERESA

Dedicated to parents who walk an unexpected road

Acknowledgments

My heart is full of love and thanks for the many people who love and pray for our family.

Thanks, Jay, for being my ballast in the storms of life. I thank God daily for you. Thanks, Taylor and Zachary, for giving me so much joy and keeping me on my knees.

Thanks, Mom, Joan and Bob, Ted and Freda, Melissa and Chris, Gaye and Eric, Jon and Londa, Jill, Corrie, Suzi, and Alison, for giving me daily support when I needed it most.

Thanks to our extended family for their much needed understanding and support.

Thanks to our church family at Calvary Fellowship, especially Allison and Amber and all the wonderful Sunday-school teachers Zack has enjoyed. Thanks to all who come up to me at church and say, "I just want you to know I'm praying for you." You have been a cup of cool water in a thirsty land for me.

Thanks to my special mom friends who share the day-to-day joys and challenges of raising children with me. It's so great to travel this road together.

Thanks to our incredible home group for years of love and friendship.

Thank you to all the amazing people who have worked with Zack throughout his short life—Dr. Shlafer, Britta, Heidi, Melissa, Lilianna, Donna, Norma, Ginny, Holly, Teri, and so many others! You are my heroes. What would we ever have done without you?

Finally, this book would not have been written without the encouragement of many people. Thanks, Bob and Linda Hayes, and the rest of the Calvary Writers Group. You not only taught me how to write but were also a great therapy group when I really needed one! Thank you especially, Nikki and Natalie, for taking care of Zack so that I could be part of the group. And thank you, Luann, for invaluable times as we meet to critique each other's work and spur one another on.

CONTENTS

NOTE

The Griffin family's story offers insight and hope to anyone experiencing or seeking to understand chronic stress and unresolved grief. Elizabeth Griffin's honest account speaks especially to those parenting or involved with children with special needs. Zack Griffin has fragile X syndrome and is among the 20 percent of people with fragile X who have autism. Because many readers may not be familiar with fragile X, we offer this definition.

fragile X—the inherited presence of a mutated gene on the X chromosome, which results in production of too little of a particular protein in the body. The results can vary widely, depending on a variety of factors, such as which generation of the mutation is present, the sex of the person, and just how much or how little of the necessary protein is produced. The effects overall are called **fragile X syndrome.** This syndrome is the most common inherited cause of mental retardation, with the degree varying in severity from relatively mild delay or impairment to severe mental retardation. Fragile X syndrome is also the most common known cause of autism. Effects can also include any of the following: specific learning disabilities, anxiety, ADHD, seizure disorders, sensory motor problems, problems with speech or language, and physical appearance characteristics particular to fragile X syndrome. A person can carry the gene without demonstrating any recognizable symptoms of its presence, and some effects, such as early menopause or a related tremor disorder, occur only in adulthood. One in 250 women is a carrier of the syndrome.

FOREWORD

Fragile X syndrome is the most common inherited cause of mental retardation known and the most common known cause of autism, and yet it is dramatically underdiagnosed. Physicians may not order the test unless they observe the typical physical features, but over 30 percent of young children with fragile X do not have prominent ears or a long face. The fragile X DNA test is easy to order, relatively inexpensive, and covered by insurance, and yet it is typically not done when a child's development is delayed. Many educators and therapists are not aware that the spectrum of involvement in fragile X is broad. Many fragile X children will have only learning disabilities (especially girls), whereas others will have autism. All children with significant delays or autism should have the fragile X DNA test done.

Elizabeth Griffin writes poignantly about her struggles to connect with her son Zack, who has autism, and her search for the cause or the etiological diagnosis, fragile X. The Griffins's frustrations are echoed throughout the world as families try to find appropriate testing, or when they are informed about the positive results of the fragile X DNA blood test, but their doctors do not know about fragile X. In this day of easy Internet access, it is often the parents who are informing the health-care professionals or the educators about the medical problems of their child. There is a wealth of information about fragile X syndrome on the Internet, perhaps the best of it under www.fragilex.org, where the National Fragile X Foundation has over twelve hundred pages ranging from medication advice to educational plans.

Elizabeth's book teaches us what we cannot find on the Internet. She tells her story from the inside; her emotions, her worries, her relationships, her instincts, and her faith are laid out in detail so that we can learn from her struggles. This is a gift not only for families but, just as importantly, for professionals so that we can improve our sensitivity to the needs of parents. Her book speaks for the millions of women worldwide who are carriers of fragile X (1 in 250 in the general population) and are struggling to connect with their children, take care of the needs of the family, and communicate with the professionals. I am amazed by their strength, and my heart is with them.

—RANDI HAGERMAN, M.D.
Professor, Department of Pediatrics;
Tsakopoulos-Vismara Chair of Pediatrics;
Medical Director of the M.I.N.D. Institute,
UC Davis Health System

PREFACE

Zack squealed with glee as I ran under the red-and-yellow swing, pushing him high into the air. I turned to face him and grabbed the swing midair.

"Ready, set, g…" I paused to let him say "Go!" and pushed again.

My boy's arms and legs flapped like a hummingbird's wings as the swing took him away from me and back again. I grabbed the swing another time, ready to say our line, when Zack surprised me with a new word, "Boo!"

Without thinking, I answered, "Don't you say 'boo,' or I'll have to tickle you!"

Zack giggled and said, "Boo!"

I tickled him and repeated my warning. He coyly laughed, "Boo!"

It was a typical interaction between a mother and her eighteen-month-old. But for us that simple game transformed a cool April morning into Christmas. Zack had just given me a life-changing gift. At age four he had played a verbal game with me for the very first time.

As I told others about our game, I felt like a little girl running around at the fair with a brightly colored balloon, sticking it in everyone's face and shouting, "See! See!" I quickly wrote to my email list, confident they would share my enthusiasm.

The first reply popped my balloon with a *pow!* "I am happy about your game with Zack, but I feel so sad that it's taken so much work and time to get to this point with him. It breaks my heart. You are very brave to be so cheerful."

My balloon shriveled and sank silently to the ground, leaving me equally deflated. We experienced so much joy in parenting Zack, despite our heartache over his limitations, but I was beginning to see that many people view children with special needs as a tragic burden.

I have to admit that prior to Zack's entrance into my life, I felt the same way. I remember hearing a speaker on the radio say he wouldn't trade the experience of having a special-needs child for anything. I thought, *Liar! You're just saying that to be positive. You don't really mean it!*

After years of working through the grief, anger, and fear that Zack's diagnosis brought, I have come to agree with the man on the radio. There's a deep sense of love and joy I've found in parenting a special-needs child that I never expected, and I'm grateful to have it in my life. Of course, it took a while to get to this place, and the beginning of that journey is where my story starts.

Chapter One

"A Late Bloomer"

I'm so afraid," I whispered in the dark.

"Afraid of what, sweetheart?" my friend asked on the other end of the phone.

I stifled a sob as tears dropped softly but steadily onto the cushion I was hugging close.

"Well, he's going to grow up, you know," I said. "What if he doesn't outgrow these delays? He won't always be cute and little."

"And that makes you afraid?" she gently queried. "What about Zack growing up frightens you?"

I paused, unsure of making my confession even to my best friend but knowing I had to share the burden of it with someone.

Corrie waited in silence.

Finally I whispered, "I'm afraid I'll stop loving him."

"Oh," she responded, then paused. "You won't. I know you won't."

"How do you know that?" I implored.

"Because I know *you*."

As we ended our conversation, I placed the phone in its cradle and crept down the hall. Turning left at the first door, I stepped in to look at Zachary. My two-year-old lay in a pool of moonlight in his crib. I watched him for a long time, memorizing the way soft curls framed his face, the peace of his velvety brow line, the soft curve of his nose. Bending over him, I drank in the apple-fresh scent of his breath.

When I came to bed, Jay turned to wrap his arm around me. I drew his hand up to cover my heart and drifted off to sleep, praying my friend was right.

♪

"Don't you think it's about time to get him off that bottle?" Dr. Brown challenged me. "That's why he keeps getting these ear infections."

"Oh, I never lay him down with a bottle," I defended myself, cringing inside.

"He'd probably talk more if he didn't always have that attached to his mouth," the on-call doctor continued. "I know it's hard for mothers. He's your youngest, isn't he?"

"Yes," I responded. "Taylor never really drank from a bottle. He went from nursing to a sippy cup. But Zack, he's different."

"And he's your baby," the doctor interrupted with a smile. "It's hard to let him grow up, but you've got to get that bottle away from him."

"I know," I mumbled. "But it's not just because he's my baby. He seems to need it right now. Somehow he seems so fragile."

EACH MENTION OF THE BOTTLE RAISED MORE BRISTLES ON MY BACK, AS IF THEY HELD ME RESPONSIBLE FOR ZACK'S CHALLENGES.

Dr. Brown smiled condescendingly, and I agreed to try harder, leaving the doctor's office with a prescription in hand for Zack's ear infection and another pound of guilt added to my backpack. Everyone was nagging me to cut Zack off from the bottle—our pediatrician, my in-laws, even on-call doctors like this one. They blamed the bottle for all his delays, as if drinking from a cup would suddenly make him walk and talk. I couldn't see the connection, and each mention of the bottle raised more bristles on my back, as if they held me responsible for Zack's challenges.

"It's not like he'll still be sucking from a bottle when he goes to kindergarten," I muttered, as Zack and I left the hospital parking lot. "They all think this is easy, like you just slam dunk the bottle into a garbage can and walk away. Ha! I wonder how long they'd withhold a bottle with their baby crying like you just cut his toes off."

I SMILED AT THE SIMPLICITY OF ZACK'S LIFE, WISHING I COULD RELAX INTO IT WITH HIM. WISHING THE SIMPLICITY COULD LAST FOREVER.

I glanced at Zack in the rearview mirror, happily sucking. His left eye winked rhythmically as he gazed dreamily out the window. Who needed anything more than a delicious bottle of milk, the steady motion of the car, and the warmth of the sun to be content and fall into a carefree slumber? I smiled at the simplicity of his life, wishing I could relax into it with him. Wishing the simplicity could last forever.

"We'll get there, buddy. You won't always be sucking on that thing," I said softly, reaching back to gently squeeze his foot.

I waited for Jay to come home before giving Zack his first dose of antibiotic. It took two of us—one to hold Zack and one to squirt the pink liquid into his screaming mouth. Jay was strong and I was fast, so we made a good combo. I squirted, then caught the sticky pink medicine with my finger as it ran down Zack's cheek and wiped it back into his mouth, silently praying that he wouldn't throw it up. If it came back up, we'd have to guess how much he actually kept down and decide whether or not to try another squirt. By the end of that simple procedure, we were all on edge.

I FELT GUILTY FOR MY BOYS'
POOR HEALTH.

That night was a restless one, since the medication hadn't started to fight the infection yet and Zack had a cold on top of it. I paced the living room with Zack, patting his back and sweating from the heat of his body against mine. Once he was asleep, I held him in the rocking chair and let my mind wander. It traveled back to a time when I was four years old.

My family had just driven four hundred miles from home on the first leg of a two-week vacation. We stopped at a hotel for the night, long after my sister and I had fallen asleep in the backseat. Daddy carried me from our car, up stairs carpeted in red shag, to a bed beneath a slanted ceiling. My body convulsed with harsh coughs as he laid me down, and the pain pulsing in my head increased with each coughing spell.

Mom lay down to sleep beside me. Awake, I lay there between her and the wall, bathed in the sweat of fever and feeling guilty. Guilty for being sick in a family that attributed physical sickness to incorrect thinking. Guilty for keeping my mother awake. Guilty at the age of four.

Thirty years later, in my own living room, I still felt guilty. Guilty that my milk didn't keep Zack immune from the common cold. Guilty that my boys had chronic ear infections and runny noses. Guilty for their poor health, just as I had been for mine as a child. Even though I had long since concluded that I couldn't get absolute control over my health by thinking a certain way, my mind was playing old tapes of the beliefs I'd been raised with, and I was too exhausted to counter them.

Our first son, Taylor, was vulnerable to ear infections, but sickness hit Zack harder as a baby. At three months he came down with a fever that brought on a seizure alarming enough to merit a trip to the emergency room. A myriad of tests showed nothing unusual, leaving us emotionally drained but relieved.

One month later, after exposure from cousins, Zack broke out with over two hundred chicken pox. His peachy soft head was covered with angry sores—beginning as small dots, swelling to adolescent-sized pimples, then bursting, draining, and scabbing over. To avoid exposing the other patients in the waiting room, I snuck my four-month-old in the back door of our naturopath's office. She declared him to have a fabulous immune system, proven by the great number of pox he had at such a young age. I guess it's all in your perspective, but I hated to see my baby so miserable.

SUFFERING ISN'T REAL UNTIL IT SHOWS UP IN YOUR OWN LIVING ROOM.

In those early months, I spent night after night pacing with Zack pressed to my chest, praying, God, *please heal my baby. Please help him sleep.* Zack would cry for hours, struggling to breathe through his clogged nose, until I was crying along with him. *I don't understand how You can let my baby suffer like this,* I would scold God, then beg, *Please, please touch his little body and make him better.*

The memory of a college classmate's voice would interrupt my prayers: "How can you pray about a common cold when babies are starving in Africa?"

We were so philosophical in those days. So proud of our worldview. Suffering isn't real until it shows up in your own living room.

Zack's sharp cry brought me back to the moment. I rocked us to sleep for a short nap before his next coughing bout. As the nights went on, these stretches of sleep would lengthen, until he recovered from his cold and I caught it.

Zack's fragility was more than physical. His connection with the world was a thin line to Jay and Taylor and me. He responded to physical touch and pleasing sounds but seldom initiated interaction with people or even with toys that other babies found fascinating, and his face was blank much of the time.

I SPENT HOURS REVIEWING MY SONS' LIVES, BUT I COULDN'T FIND A REASON FOR THESE DIFFERENCES.

Our pediatrician, Dr. Hanson, repeatedly assured me that everything was fine. "Zack is at the slow end of the scale, but he isn't off it yet" was his standard answer to my concerns. I waited for the doctor to take action, hoping he was right.

In the meantime I tried not to compare my boys. Taylor had walked at ten months and talked at eleven. At twice that age, Zack could barely sit on his own, wasn't walking, and couldn't verbalize except to make growling noises.

I spent hours reviewing my sons' lives, but I couldn't find a reason for these differences. Maybe our pediatrician was right and I was obsessing needlessly. But maybe, just maybe, there was a problem that I needed to do something about.

♪ *Long before any human being saw us, we are seen by God's loving eyes. Long before anyone heard us cry or laugh, we are heard by our God who is all ears for us. Long before any person spoke to us in this world, we are spoken to by the voice of eternal love. Our preciousness, uniqueness and individuality are not given to us by those who meet us in clock-time—our brief chronological existence—but by the One who has chosen us with an everlasting love, a love that existed from all eternity and will last through all eternity.*

—Henri J. M. Nouwen[1]

♪ *For you created my inmost being; you knit me together in my mother's womb. I praise you because I am fearfully and wonderfully made; your works are wonderful, I know that full well. My frame was not hidden from you when I was made in the secret place. When I was woven together in the depths of the earth, your eyes saw my unformed body. All the days ordained for me were written in your book before one of them came to be. How precious to me are your thoughts, O God! How vast is the sum of them! Were I to count them, they would outnumber the grains of sand. When I awake, I am still with you.*

—Psalm 139:13–18

✎ Chapter Two

DESPERATE
FOR SOMEONE TO LISTEN

I tried to catch Zack's eye as we sat eating crackers at the kitchen table. He looked past me and smiled, as if he saw another world. He waved his arms and cheerfully addressed a crowd invisible to me, in a language I didn't understand. I shivered in the loneliness of not being seen. I thought back to the night before when he wouldn't go to sleep until he lay on top of me. His tiny hand had slowly unclenched and spread out flat as his body relaxed into mine. I remembered the warmth of him on my chest and clung to it in the coldness of this present isolation. Moments like that were my anchor of hope that we had a connection, that there was a place for me in his world.

It was around Zack's first birthday that shadows began forming at the edges of our cloudless universe. Until then he was Taylor's delightful opposite. Sure, he was much slower in development, but our firstborn had done everything at record speed. We figured Zack was just on his own timetable.

I taped a copy of Psalm 139 beside Zack's crib and read it often, especially the part that said, "For you created my inmost being; you knit me together in my mother's womb. I praise you because I am fearfully and wonderfully made!" I was working overtime to fight the nameless worries I felt rising in my heart.

We were thrilled when Zack could sit up. I placed him in front of his brightly colored Sesame Street baby gym to watch him play.

"Here's Elmo," I singsonged as I swung his favorite character.

"Aaaaaaaaaaaaaaaaahhhhhhhh," he responded, his arms up and his fists shaking back and forth.

"It's okay, baby. You can grab Elmo. Go for it, love," I encouraged him.

Zack leaned forward with enthusiasm, shaking his arms vigorously and repeating "Aaaaaaaaaaaaaaaahhhhhhhhh."

"Sweetie, grab him." My voice shook like Zack's arms, emerging worries gripping at my throat.

"Aaaaaaaaaaaaaaaaahhhhhhhh."

Finally, one day, as Zack's arms shook, seemingly stuck in a repetitive cycle that kept him from grabbing the toy, I touched him. His hand immediately reached out and grabbed Elmo as if a circuit had connected from his brain to his hand.

"Yes, yes, Zack. That's it! That's Elmo," I sang, delighted with the breakthrough.

I raced to tell Jay when he walked through the door that night. "Yay, Zack!" Jay cheered, "I knew you could do it!" Then, turning to me with a hug, he said, "See, honey, he's getting there. He's gonna be okay."

The next day we started the game all over again. And the next day, and the next. Months passed without further progress.

I shared worries long distance with my mother and sister. "His hand movements are like the reflexes a baby has, but he's over a year old. He doesn't turn to his name when I say it, but if I sing it he looks at me and smiles. He never reaches out and grabs what he wants. I just know he wants it because his arms shake and he says, 'Aaaaaaaaaaahhhhhhhhhhh.'"

Mom sent me information on autism. I filled out paper-and-pencil tests and determined that Zack was on the spectrum. Our pediatrician said to give Zack time, that his attachment to me was too strong for him to be autistic.

BY THIS TIME MOST OF THE FAMILY WAS ON EDGE ABOUT ZACK'S DEVELOPMENT BUT NOT SURE HOW TO BROACH THE SUBJECT WITH JAY AND ME.

By this time most of the family was on edge about Zack's development but not sure how to broach the subject with Jay and me.

"I'm sure he'll walk any day now," I would answer my mother-in-law's questions. "He actually took a few steps yesterday."

It was true, he had taken steps the day before, but he didn't again for a week. Then he took a few more steps, and we spent another week waiting for him to walk again. This went on for four months before he consistently walked.

One day during a play date, before Zack was walking on his own, a friend asked, "How old would you say Zack is developmentally right now?"

I looked at my twenty-month-old as he sat unusually still and quiet on their living-room floor, ignoring the bright toys that surrounded him. "I've been thinking that he's about twelve months," I said.

"Yeah, that's about what I'd say," Terry replied. "You know, we have such great resources in this city. You might want to check with Children's Hospital and see what they say about Zack's development, just for your own peace of mind."

Emboldened by his words, I made an appointment with our pediatrician for a developmental assessment. With Joan, my mother-in-law, by my side, I listened while the doctor asked question after question.

"No, Zack is not walking independently."

"No, Zack does not respond to his name."

"No, Zack is not saying any words at all."

No. No. No. Haven't I been telling you this for months? I screamed inside my head.

Dr. Hanson concluded, "Well, he's at about twelve months on the charts. Still, I suspect there's nothing seriously wrong. But a little therapy couldn't hurt, so why don't I set up appointments for some evaluations?"

The promised appointments were never scheduled. Two months later I heard about a "Birth to Three" center, where I took Zack to begin therapy immediately. He was twenty-two months old.

I WANTED SOMEONE TO THROW ME A LIFELINE, TO HELP SOLVE THE MYSTERY OF MY CHILD'S BEHAVIOR.

Fueled by fury against the medical community and my passive acceptance of their conclusions, I searched for answers to questions I'd been afraid to ask. I wanted someone to throw me a lifeline, to help solve the mystery of my child's behavior. None came, only phantom lines that disappeared when I reached to grab them.

We went to a neurologist recommended by a friend of the family. A specialist on seizures, she ordered an EEG that proved Zack didn't have seizures and an MRI that showed that his brain looked normal. We were on her books for a follow-up appointment in three weeks.

Then a clue to our puzzle came from an unexpected source. Suspecting I was pregnant, I went to my gynecologist only to find out I was in early menopause.

"Can I give you a reason?" he said. "I have no idea why this happened. It could be stress or postpregnancy issues. There's a small chance it could be some quirk on your X chromosome that will never show up in any other way than this, but that's so unlikely it's hardly worth mentioning."

I IMAGINED THREE CHILDREN, ALL PERFECTLY HEALTHY AND BRILLIANT. REALITY WAS RUINING MY PLANS.

This news of early menopause was a second threat to my dream family. I imagined three children, all perfectly healthy and brilliant. I had the two boys, and the girl would be coming next. She would have curly blond hair and huge blue eyes, just like her brothers. Reality was ruining my plans.

It became very important for us to know if genetics played a part in Zack's delays. Time may have run out for me to conceive again, but there was always a chance. However, if Zack's condition was inherited, we would reconsider having a third child.

Desperate for someone to listen and give us answers, we changed pediatricians. A week before our first appointment with Dr. Shlafer, I ran into an acquaintance at Zack's therapy center. We talked in the parking lot after dropping off our boys, and she told me about her son's diagnosis of "fragile X syndrome."

The "X" triggered my memory. Could there be a connection between my early menopause and Zack's condition? I would soon learn that 20 percent of carriers of fragile X syndrome go through early menopause. All I knew then was that as she listed the syndrome's characteristics, she was describing Zack.

I searched Internet Web sites about fragile X syndrome, praying, *Oh God, please don't let this be it. Please, please, anything but this.*

If it was fragile X syndrome, then it was genetic, inherited from me. That meant no more babies. And Zack would never get better.

I arrived at Zack's first appointment with Dr. Shlafer, armed and ready to plead our case.

"Zack is very delayed in development. He's twenty-six months old and not talking yet," I began.

"What did the metabolic and chromosomal workup show about him?" the doctor interrupted.

"What?" I questioned. "I'm sorry. What is a metabolic and chromosomal workup? I've never heard of this before."

"You mean, no one has ever done a neurological screening on Zack?" he asked.

"A what? I'm sorry, I have no idea what you're talking about. Does that mean an EEG and MRI? He's had those."

Dr. Shlafer frowned. "I wonder why they did those," he mumbled, then said, "Mrs. Griffin, the first thing that should be done with a child who has delays like Zack's is a metabolic and chromosomal workup. Are you telling me that no one has ever suggested this to you before?"

"Yes, that's what I'm telling you. I didn't know...." My voice quavered as residual guilt crept in.

"Of course you didn't know, Mrs. Griffin. That's the doctor's job. That's what you pay us for," he said, shaking his head.

I wanted to throw my arms around this man and sob on his shoulder in relief, but I only nodded silently and thanked God for him.

"If you would like, I will order these tests immediately," he offered. "Or your neurologist can take them on your follow-up appointment. Didn't you say you were seeing her soon?"

"Yes, I guess I'll have her do it," I said, thinking it would be faster that way.

"Have her send me the results immediately, and call me if I can help in any other way in the meantime." Dr. Shlafer shook my hand to conclude our appointment.

When Jay, his mother, Joan, and I met with the neurologist the next week, she said, "It's virtually impossible for Zack to have fragile X syndrome. Children with fragile X syndrome have long faces and large ears. Zack simply does not have the look of fragile X."

"But he has many of the characteristics of the syndrome," I countered.

"I can almost guarantee you he doesn't have it. But if you insist, we can run the blood test."

SINCE I ASSUMED SHE KNEW MORE THAN I DID, MY CONFIDENCE WAVERED. I SUSPECTED I WAS RIGHT, BUT I COULDN'T PROVE IT.

If I'd known more about the syndrome, I could have told her that it isn't until puberty that most people with fragile X syndrome have what she called "the look." Since I didn't know that, and I assumed she knew more than I did, my confidence wavered. I suspected I was right, but I couldn't prove it. I needed support, so I decided to go back to the only doctor who would listen to me. "That's all right," I said, "we'll have our pediatrician take care of the testing."

As we left the doctor's office, Joan put her arm around my shoulders and gently chided me for doing "layman's research," suggesting I leave the diagnosing in professional hands. She and Jay agreed that my Internet findings had only resulted in unnecessary anguish.

Zack and I took the elevator to the parking garage as Jay returned to work and Joan went home. I drove away, my mind spinning in circles like Zack's tightfisted hands and my ears humming with the sound of the only word he knew, "Aaaaaahhhhhhhhh."

Be at peace—
Do not fear the changes of life—
Rather look to them with full hope as they arise.

God, whose very own you are,
will deliver you from out of them.
He has kept you hitherto,
and He will lead you safely through all things;
and when you cannot stand it,
God will bury you in His arms.

Do not be afraid of what may happen tomorrow;
the same everlasting Father who cares for you today
will take care of you then and every day.

He will either shield you from suffering,
or will give you unfailing strength to bear it.

Be at peace—
and put aside all anxious thoughts and imaginations.

—ST. FRANCIS DE SALES (1567–1622)

The LORD *will fulfill his purpose for me; your love, O* LORD, *endures forever—do not abandon the works of your hands.*

—PSALM 138:8

DIAGNOSIS

Mrs. Griffin, this is Dr. Shlafer. Your son has fragile X syndrome."

I laughed nervously into the phone. He must be kidding.

"Didn't the tests all come back normal?" I asked, remembering how we'd checked off each test with relief as its results came back over the past three months.

"Actually, no. We were waiting for one last test, and it showed that Zack is fragile X positive. I'd like you to come in as soon as possible."

After hanging up, I sat down and held my head, trying to remember to breathe. I dialed Jay's cell phone and told him flatly, just as the doctor had told me. He came home immediately.

We went into the pediatrician's office to hear basic facts about the syndrome: most children with fragile X learn to talk with extensive speech therapy; most are potty-trained; Zack is likely to progress until puberty, and then his development will slow down or stop; he will probably never live independently; he is among the 20 percent of people with fragile X who have autism.

Back home, Jay and I went through the motions of dinner and bedtime reading to the boys, feeling as if we were on the outside looking in on someone else's life and wishing that were true.

JAY CONTINUED ON, REPEATING THINGS I HAD BEEN SAYING TO HIM FOR MONTHS. I WAS DUMBFOUNDED. *HADN'T HE BEEN LISTENING TO ME?*

After a night of fitful sleep, Jay got up at 4:30 to go to work. He sat on the side of the bed, thinking, and finally began to talk. "We need to get Zack into therapy, Elizabeth. We need to do everything we can for him. He needs speech therapy and physical therapy and… we need to stimulate him more at home, to make him look us in the eyes." Jay continued on, repeating things I had been saying to him for months.

I was dumbfounded. *Hadn't he been listening to me? Didn't he know I was doing all of these things already?* My heart raced toward fury, but then I suddenly understood. "I get it," I said slowly. "You didn't believe there was a problem before now, did you?"

"No," Jay said. "I thought he'd outgrow it. I never thought it was real until now."

We held each other and cried. I looked at my husband in the darkness of that morning and knew I needed him desperately. "Nothing can ever happen to you," I whispered, almost as a prayer.

"I know," he said. "We really need each other."

Having a diagnosis was beneficial for many reasons: it united Jay and me in our care for Zack, it helped extended family and friends grasp the challenges we faced, and it gave us access to school and government programs. Important doors that had been closed were now opening.

I reminded myself daily that it was good to have a diagnosis.

But in the weeks following Zack's diagnosis, sadness settled into my bones. Like sand filling every nook and cranny between rocks, it permeated my life. A friend offered to take the boys so I could escape to a matinee. Once in the darkened theater, I sobbed through two romantic comedies. Jay and I went to an upbeat concert by my favorite singing group, and I sat numbly waiting for it to end. Every event intended to distract me from reality only highlighted my heartache. Even worshiping at church, singing "Oh Happy Day," made me cry. It would be several years before I could enjoy a simple outing again.

ZACK WASN'T JUST A LATE BLOOMER; HE WAS SEVERELY IMPAIRED. HIS LIFE WOULD NEVER BE WHAT I HAD IMAGINED IT TO BE, NOR WOULD MINE.

When I looked at Zack, I knew that the diagnosis hadn't changed anything. He was still as sweet as could be, with his quirky behaviors we had found charming and unique before this new label was slapped on them. But now I knew he wouldn't outgrow these idiosyncrasies. He wasn't just a late bloomer; he was severely impaired. His life would never be what I had imagined it to be, nor would mine.

"Ahhhh." I sat up in bed, my back prickling with fear over a nightmarish image of Zack rocking and groaning. Trying to shake off sleep, I brushed hair back from my moist forehead. "Oh God, help me," I gasped as reality sank in.

I felt fear's tentacles suction onto my heart. Without warning, they tightened their grip and yanked me under. I reached out to Jay, tears streaming down my cheeks.

I am here with you, came the whisper in my heart. *I am never going to leave you. I will carry you through this.*

I'm drowning, Lord. I can't. I'm so afraid. I want to die.

When you pass through the waters, I will be there. I will not let you drown, Elizabeth. I am with you in this. Trust me.

I took deep, shuddering breaths, slowly soaking in the words of life. Sleep came for a few more hours.

Waking at 3:00 A.M., however, would become a nightly part of my life. Night after night Jay would hold me while I cried, or I would slip out of bed and kneel in the living room, crying out for peace. My thoughts were consumed with death—dreading that all my physical aches and extreme exhaustion were caused by cancer and then wishing that they were.

EXHAUSTION SPILLED INTO MY DAYS, MAKING IT IMPOSSIBLE FOR ME TO CONTROL MY EMOTIONS. I CRIED ENDLESSLY, WITHOUT ANY APPARENT REASON. MY FEARS GENERALIZED.

Exhaustion spilled into my days, making it impossible for me to control my emotions. I cried endlessly, without any apparent reason. My fears generalized. Would Jay die? Would Taylor be stolen from me?

I marched through each day, checking off my to-do list, but inside I was fighting with all my strength not to shriek and howl, rip everything off the walls of our house, and end up rocking with Zack in the corner.

My doctor listened with compassion, then said, "Elizabeth, you are under a tremendous amount of stress. I want to put you on some medication that will help you sleep and another one to deal with this anxiety."

"Do you really think I need it?" I asked. "I'm just not sure."

"It's up to you, but yes, I really think you need it," she affirmed.

"I think I'll try to work it out another way," I said, going home with a hopelessness in my heart that I resolved to push through.

I was raised to see medication as an unnecessary evil that prevents our spiritual growth. Even as a Christian I had always believed that if I trusted God enough, I would have peace in any circumstance. To take an antidepressant was to say that God wasn't big enough, to fail in my faith, to cop out. As desperate as I felt, I wouldn't let myself be helped by human invention. I felt like I had to get through this with just God and me.

So where do you go when you can't fix your life? The only place to go is back to the One who made you. You have a divine destiny, a purpose from God that no one else can fulfill. It begins with a risk. We have to find the courage to take all the pieces of our lives, our hopes and dreams back to the One who made us—and ask Him who we are. Then He, like the watchmaker, will carefully and gently replace our broken parts, showing us what we are meant to be and giving us all that we need to live according to our purpose and His plan.

—SHEILA WALSH[1]

I lift up my eyes to the hills—where does my help come from? My help comes from the LORD, the Maker of heaven and earth. He will not let your foot slip—he who watches over you will not slumber; indeed, he who watches over Israel will neither slumber nor sleep. The LORD watches over you—the LORD is your shade at your right hand; the sun will not harm you by day, nor the moon by night. The LORD will keep you from all harm—he will watch over your life; the LORD will watch over your coming and going both now and forevermore.

—PSALM 121

TICKLED BY ANGELS

You walk around the yard and talk to the wind,
raising your hands and rejoicing in your fingers.
Every now and then you laugh out loud,
a delicious giggle that comes so easily
I wonder if there are angels tickling your ribs.
Oh, to see what you see
for just a moment.
What is it you see, my love?
Do you see heaven, do you see angels,
while I am earthbound and see only you?
My vision is so limited.
I see a few feet ahead
and purposely try to keep it that way,
so I will not fret over what is not yet here,
while you have not a care in this world.
Your God watches over you.
Surely the sun will not harm you by day
nor the moon by night.
He will be the shade at your right hand,
He will watch over your life.
He tousles your curls
and kisses your face with His wind.
Speaking words of love through
the sunshine that warms your frame,
He is forever calling out your name.
You hear Him
while I watch every move,
praying for signs you are becoming
more a part of my world,
wanting it to be my voice you hear.

—ELIZABETH GRIFFIN

Chapter Four

THERAPY: ONE MORE SKILL, ONE MORE CONNECTION

I sat at the seminar on autism, numbly taking notes. Getting out of bed each morning was a monumental challenge for me, not to mention surviving the day. Now I was being told to create specialized games and toys and use them in play with my child with the promise that this would build bridges of communication between us. I was too exhausted to communicate with anyone, let alone a toddler who screamed with annoyance every time I tried to interrupt his solitude.

I drove home, tears blurring my vision like the rain on my windshield.

God, You've given Zack the wrong mother. You know I'm a random, global thinker. I can't do this concrete, sequential stuff. Do you hear me? I CAN'T DO THIS!!! No wonder I feel so incompetent. He needs someone organized, not me!

It seemed like a cruel joke. I had a teaching certificate, but I wasn't qualified to teach my own child. I had no idea how to start with him, even after listening to a two-hour lecture on a surefire, step-by-step method that guaranteed great results. It was hopeless. I walked into the dark house and went straight to bed.

Soon after this, I read a book about a mother who cured her two children of autism within a few years by using a particular therapy called applied behavioral analysis, or ABA. That mother had a full-time therapist for her children, and they weren't affected by fragile X syndrome, but I overlooked that part and was ready to jump onboard. In May we took Zack to a local center that specialized in this therapy.

HEARING OUR LITTLE BOY SAY "BUBBLE" WAS WORTH PAYING ONE AND A HALF TIMES OUR MORTGAGE FOR THERAPY EACH MONTH.

Jay, my mother-in-law, Joan, and I watched hopefully as the director of the center got Zack to repeat her words within minutes. Her three-ring-circus act of bubbles, balls, and balloons enthralled him. We were dazzled, too, sure he would be talking in full sentences by Christmas.

We signed up and left with tears of hope in our eyes. The price didn't matter at this point. Hearing our little boy say "bubble" was worth paying one and a half times our mortgage for therapy each month. Joan was willing to help cover the cost, and I went back to work to bring in more. We rented out our family room to a student for the balance.

I naively expected everyone's full support in our therapy choices and their loud applause for the sacrifices we were making to help our child, so it threw me off guard when the director of Zack's Birth-to-Three program suddenly turned a cold shoulder to my little boy. Previously friendly with him, she had no patience for helping him adjust to a schedule that included outside therapy. The instant he cried, she assumed he was exhausted and called me to take him home.

Already guilt-ridden about my two-and-a-half-year-old working so hard each day, I took Zack out of the preschool program for a few months so that we could concentrate on the ABA therapy. This, too, was a big mistake in the Birth-to-Three director's opinion.

I had no idea such opinionated camps existed regarding therapy for autism and related conditions. Though many professionals welcome any technique that helps a child, some regard any but the one they have trained in with alert suspicion. It can be like two armies, standing on opposite banks of a river armed and ready for battle. The territories are well marked, and those foolish enough to think there might be benefit in more than one approach are in danger of getting caught in the crossfire. We had entered the danger zone.

IN A FEW SHORT PHRASES, SHE HAD DISMISSED MY THREE-YEAR-OLD AS A HOPELESS CASE. IT WAS AS IF SHE WERE NAILING A LID ON THE BOX ZACK WAS IN AND SENDING HIM OFF TO STORAGE.

Within a few months Zack was used to his ABA schedule and went back to his Birth-to-Three preschool center for the summer. The session went swimmingly, but as we prepared for him to transfer to developmental preschool that fall, I was once again broad-sided by the director's attitude.

At Zack's final evaluation, she summed up her opinion in a few icy sentences. "Well, Zack has not made much progress here. I'm not sure what to tell you. The only suggestion I can give is that you find an aide somewhere who might be able to do something with him."

In a few short phrases, she had dismissed my three-year-old as a hopeless case. It was as if she were nailing a lid on the box Zack was in and sending him off to storage. Her comments ignited molten lava in my heart. Before it had a chance to boil over, I made a hasty exit and headed for a good friend's house. There I repeated the director's cruel words through sobs of pain and fury.

Alison didn't say much; she just listened with compassion to my story. Then she prayed for me.

I went home and called my mom, again repeating the poisonous words. Mom, a registered nurse, explained, "The comments are because of professional jealousy more than anything else. They aren't about Zack as much as they are the director's way of discounting the ABA therapy. Try not to let them fester, dear. Just let it go, and don't let yourself get bitter."

After raging for another day, I wrote the director a letter. Then I tore it up and threw it away. I wrote another one and considered sending it, but tore it up too. I couldn't follow Mom's advice. My heart was already a few miles down the road to bitterness.

Lord, I prayed, *I hate this woman for what she said. How dare she? But I know I can't keep being angry or I'll just sink deeper into the pit I'm already in. I can't afford to get more depressed. Please help.*

I felt no great change of heart, but a few days later I wrote a letter listing the progress we had seen in Zack during the past year and thanking the staff for helping him. I wouldn't be defeated by one woman's unkind words. Zack had made progress and would continue to, regardless of what anyone said.

We continued the ABA therapy for almost a year. By that point Zack had learned how to imitate people, the essential skill for learning that he'd been missing. He was able to sit in a small group and participate in songs and listen to books. He had also learned to give us pictures to tell us what he needed and to communicate with a few signs and words. It was incredible progress, and I would have continued the therapy forever, but it was too great a drain on our budget.

We switched to a much less expensive, home-based therapy. Heidi came with her magical box of goodies several times a week and, captivating Zack, worked with him for the next year. What she did proved to be even more effective for him.

Through Heidi we learned about listening and movement therapy. These movement sessions improved Zack's balance and coordination immensely, something which, according to the theory behind the therapy, was the basis of language development. Once again my hopes that my boy would eventually talk soared high.

TO ME, EVERYTHING ZACK LEARNED WAS PRICELESS. EVERYTHING THAT MADE IT EASIER FOR US TO CONNECT WAS PURE GOLD.

Every penny I could beg, borrow, or earn went straight to therapy, and we tried several more kinds. Jay and I spent hours discussing the value of each one.

Our conversations usually began with my relaying some exciting progress made that day and adding, "This therapy really seems to help."

"Yes, but maybe he's just growing up," Jay would counter. "Do you really think it's the therapy, or would Zack be changing in these ways without it?"

"I don't know," I would sigh. "I'm just not willing to risk not doing it."

"I know, honey, but we're sinking financially," he'd point out.

"Jay, I know. I just…don't you think Zack's worth it?"

"Of course Zack's worth it, Elizabeth. You know that's not what I'm saying. It's just that I wonder if we're throwing our money away on all this therapy."

"I know. I wonder, too."

I wondered, but I also knew deep inside that I would keep pushing for every last minute of therapy we could do. I didn't care if we went bankrupt; this was my baby, and I couldn't stop therapy if continuing meant one more skill learned or one more moment of the connection with him that I longed for. To me, everything Zack learned was priceless—every little, seemingly insignificant skill. Everything that made it easier for us to connect was pure gold.

I SIMPLY COULDN'T CONTROL ZACK'S PROGRESS.

Oh, God, I prayed many times. *Why did you give Zack to a family that lives on a tight budget? Why couldn't you have given him to millionaires who could afford all the therapy in the world? Why us?*

Although therapy had become my hope for Zack's future, eventually I saw that I had to let it go. The "if only we'd done this earlier!" guilt that each new method brought, the obsessive search for a solution to my little boy's problems, and the fear of missing the golden key to his development were enough to drive me crazy. I simply couldn't control Zack's progress, and though therapy helped, it wasn't a guarantee that he would ever catch up with his peers.

Fortunately, as Zack got older, public school began to fill in where therapy left off. When Zack turned six, he qualified for a class that provided intense communication therapy in a setting of one adult to every two children, for five and a half hours a day. That was better than any therapeutic program I could have put together on my own.

In time I have found that the key to Zack's development is working with professionals who enjoy what they are doing, are fond of my child, and have hope for his future. These are the people who make appropriate demands on him and who are patient enough to give him the time to meet their expectations. Whether through private therapy or in a public-school setting, it is in situations that both support and challenge him that Zack responds and grows.

.♪ *Face your deficiencies and acknowledge them; but do not let them master you. Let them teach you patience, sweetness, insight. When we do the best we can, we never know what miracle is wrought in our life, or in the life of another.*

—HELEN KELLER

.♪ *Therefore, strengthen your feeble arms and weak knees. "Make level paths for your feet," so that the lame may not be disabled, but rather healed.*

—HEBREWS 12:12–13

⸌ Chapter Five

SPECIAL MOMS CLUB

I don't remember getting the registration forms in the mail or filling them out, but somehow I was a member of a new club. It was like those mail-order book clubs where the monthly selection automatically comes unless you mark "no" in eight places and put the stamp precisely in the upper right corner of the envelope. I hadn't meant to join. I didn't want to join. And yet I found myself meeting with club members in waiting rooms all across the city.

I got the feeling that most of the members in this club didn't want to be in it any more than I did. They sat with "Exceptional Child" magazines pressed up to their noses, blocking out the world, while their children spent an expensive hour behind closed doors. Most members looked exhausted, rarely spoke, and had no visible social life.

I missed my old club, the one with happy mommies in it who chased their toddlers around the playground and were quick to compare stories of nursing and teething and first words. I didn't have time to go to those club meetings anymore. So I sat in waiting rooms, feeling lonely, resolving not to be depressed, not to ignore my children, and not to hide behind magazines.

It took months before I got a look into the eyes of the other members of this club. What I saw, beyond the exhaustion, were tenacious mother bears. Sure, they took a break in the waiting room, but it was a well-earned one. It recharged them for the interaction they would be catapulted into when that therapist's door opened and their children charged out. I saw their wisdom soon enough and escaped into a few magazines myself.

As I made some connections with these moms, my respect for them grew. We were a club with lifetime membership, and, boy, did we have stories to tell.

"IT'S NEVER EASY, BUT THERE IS JOY ALONG THE WAY."

Lori, our initial caseworker from the Division of Developmental Disabilities, was among the first to share her story with me. Lori has three sons, the oldest one severely autistic. Her husband left eighteen years ago, when the boys were all toddlers. On her first visit to our home, she told me about the stages her oldest son had gone through: the poop smearing stage, the spitting stage, the screeching stage.

After her detailed account, she sighed. "My son will be moving into a group home next month, and it sure is going to be quiet. I'll miss him."

I sat in silent amazement at her words. Missing him was the last thing I thought she'd say.

As Lori was leaving our home that day, I groped for some tangible straw of encouragement. Tentatively, I asked, "Does it ever, you know, get easier?"

She paused, then thoughtfully replied, "It's never easy, but there is joy along the way."

Lori's story was not the only one to surprise and inspire me. I was waiting for Zack's therapy to end one day when a couple wheeled their son into the waiting room. He was about the size of a fifteen-year-old. Awkwardly placed in a wheelchair, his arms and legs were stiff and twisted at the wrists and ankles. One hand was near his face, jerking occasionally. He leaned to one side, his head tilted and his jaw askew. Drool flowed over his crooked teeth and down his chin.

THE GLOW IN THEIR EYES WAS UNMISTAKABLE! THEY REALLY LOVED HIM! THERE WAS NO DOUBT ABOUT IT.

The couple sat down and turned his chair to face them. From my vantage point across the room, I watched them looking at him and conversing. He stared into space, giving no indication that he heard them. Yet they continued to speak to him in lively, interesting tones. I was intrigued. The glow in their eyes was unmistakable! They really loved him! There was no doubt about it.

As I became aware of other people's stories, it didn't take long for me to open my own branch of the "Special Moms Club." Noticing several potential members at church, I thought we needed to get to know each other. I put a notice in the bulletin one Sunday, and six women responded. We told our stories and prayed together. The group decided to meet every week.

With a Bible study as our framework, we spent hours talking about God's role as Creator of our children, expressing our emotions in response to having a child with special needs, and pondering what God was requiring of us in this role. We asked questions freely: Is it wrong to be angry with God? Is it okay to grieve for years? Is there an appropriate and an inappropriate response to pain and suffering?

We didn't come to definite conclusions, but we all agreed that emotions were neutral—neither good nor bad—and that it was our *attitude* toward God in the midst of our circumstances that mattered. It was all right to struggle with God but not to walk away from Him.

One day, after our December break from meeting, each one of us came straggling in. I was surprised at the crises that had occurred in all six of our lives during the three weeks we had not met. New medications, further diagnoses, irrational behavior, and poor sleeping patterns in our kids had left us all ragged. A few minutes into our meeting we decided to skip the Bible study and go right to prayer.

MY TIME WITH THESE WOMEN REINFORCED MY CONVICTION THAT EVERY MOM NEEDS PEOPLE SHE CAN SPEAK HER HEART TO WITHOUT FEAR OF JUDGMENT.

In our circle, we understood each other without explanations. Though our children's disabilities were varied, our heartache, frustration, and exhaustion were universal. We sought out each other's nuggets of expertise to help us understand our children—both typically developed and disabled. No matter the subject, from deciding which school program was right for our child to surviving visits from extended family, we laughed and cried and prayed together. The rest of our week was easier because of Wednesday mornings.

My time with these women reinforced my conviction that every mom needs people she can speak her heart to without fear of judgment. Some people find this support through professional

I FOUND THAT GETTING TO THE CORE OF MY SADNESS NEVER HAPPENED DURING NORMAL WORKING HOURS.

therapy. It is helpful for them to discuss problems with a professional, someone who is removed from the situation, rather than someone closely connected. Others find it through friends and family. I tried both and found that getting to the core of my sadness never happened during normal working hours.

It was midnight when I curled up at my mother's feet in our guest room and began to whimper. Zack had cried for hours that evening, convulsing hysterically, until now he was finally asleep in my bedroom.

"Does Zack often cry like that?" Mom asked softly.

"No. He's never done this before. Do you think it's a seizure?"

"I don't know, darling. I think maybe the day was just too much for him."

"And for me," I added. Hours in traffic during an August heat wave, plus a full day of visiting with relatives and friends, equaled nothing but stress for a little boy who only wanted to be home in his own backyard. Add too many glasses of juice and handfuls of crackers, which led to the inevitable scene of Zack throwing up on the shiny tile floor of my mother's best friend's completely white kitchen, and we were over the top. I still smelled like vomit, even after washing my hands half a dozen times.

Mom reached down and stroked my hair.

I began to talk about the two weeks prior to her arrival. We had finished our first twelve-day round of Tomatis therapy the day before her visit. The therapy required Zack to wear a heavy set of head phones for two hours each day and listen to modified Mozart. Most of us would love to relax and tune out the world in this way, but for a five-year-old who can't stand to have any-thing touch his ears, it was excruciating. Zack and I engaged in two-hour wrestling matches each day at the therapy center as he struggled to remove the head phones and I repeatedly put them back on him. By the end of the session, I was hanging on by a thread of faith that this therapy would somehow help my son integrate the sensory input that bombarded him every day. Mak-ing sense of this input would increase Zack's receptive language skills, which in turn would, eventually, lead to talking—the promised goal of this outrageously priced, experimental therapy.

THESE CHILDREN SAT QUIETLY PUTTING LEGOS TOGETHER, WHILE MY SON THRASHED ABOUT, DEMANDING AN UNENDING SUPPLY OF ENERGY AND STRENGTH I COULD NOT GIVE.

Mom commiserated with my exhaustion after running such a marathon. I continued to tell her about the other children we had seen there, all of whom were miles ahead of Zack develop-mentally. As I spoke, my emotions bubbled to the surface, includ-ing doubts about the therapy's effectiveness and the agony of comparing my son with other children whose mothers simply dropped them off and shopped during their sessions. These chil-dren sat quietly putting Legos together as they listened to music, while my son thrashed about, demanding an unending supply of energy and strength I could not give.

I told Mom about one woman I met who brought her son because he was slightly behind in his first-grade class. Apparently her entire neighborhood was going through the therapy with their children, so she figured she'd give it a go.

"Her son doesn't even *need* therapy, but they have so much money they can afford to do it without a second thought. And here we are, desperate for something to help Zack, just wanting a few words from him, and we can barely scrape together enough to pay for it."

"Oh, honey, it just isn't fair, is it?"

"I guess I'd do the same if I were her. I mean, I'd do anything to help my child, but it's just so hard for us," I sobbed. "I don't even know if it'll do any good. It could all be a waste of time and money."

A GREAT WAVE OF GRIEF WELLED
UP INSIDE OF ME. MY VOICE WAS
LOUD, BUT I COULDN'T STOP NOW.

Mom groaned in sympathy. "There must be something that can be done for a child like this. Don't they have places for children like Zack?" she asked.

For a horrible instant I considered her words. Was she suggesting putting Zack in a home? Would I actually consider doing such a thing? Even to think of the possibility felt like high treason, the most treacherous of all betrayals.

"He's my baby..." I sobbed uncontrollably, as I began rocking back and forth. "My baby," I groaned, "my baby."

A great wave of grief welled up inside of me like an ocean swell in a winter storm. My voice was loud, and I knew it might wake my boys in the next room, but I couldn't stop now. I had tried to express this grief in expensive therapy sessions of my own and couldn't. What I'd needed was the right moment— utter exhaustion after a day of heat and polite conversation, then coming home to Zack crying hysterically for hours. Combined with Mom quietly asking questions, responding with appropriate "hmms" and "ahhs" to my ramblings, and letting me bawl, it was the perfect catalyst for a breakdown.

"It's a real test of faith," Mom quietly murmured.

♪ *Oh, the comfort, the inexpressible comfort of feeling safe with a person: having neither to weigh thoughts nor measure words, but to pour them out.*

—GEORGE ELIOT (MARY ANN EVANS)[1]

♪ *A friend loves at all times, and a brother is born for adversity.*

—PROVERBS 17:17

⌒ Chapter Six

MOURNING WITHOUT BOUNDARY: UNRESOLVED GRIEF

I couldn't get a deep enough breath. Daily I carried grief's full weight up an endless flight of stairs. I couldn't run from its source, my little Zack. There was no respite from being his mommy.

"Honeeeee, Honeeeee!" The wail comes from the depths of Zack's soul, accompanied by copious tears.

"It's okay, baby. Mommy be right back," I reply, my voice pleading with Zack to calm down. "Look. You can still see Mommy." I put my face up to the window he peers through anxiously. "Mommy's just going right here. I'm right here."

Slowly I back up toward the mailbox, or to close the gate on our driveway, or turn to race to the video drop-off box, hurrying to complete tasks that take me away from Zack for less than a few minutes. But they are excruciating minutes for him, trapped in his car seat and desperate to keep his security in view.

"Zack, it's okay," moans Taylor, sitting next to him. "See, she's just dropping off a video."

Talking sense doesn't help. Zack cries long after I've returned and we're speeding on our way. We will comfort him with hugs and kisses, try to distract him with books and candy, and finally just have to wait for enough time to pass that he calms down.

I BECAME ANGRY. ANGRY BECAUSE I DIDN'T WANT TO BE SAD ANYMORE.

Anxiety—I've lived with it my entire life as a carrier of fragile X, but my boy suffers from it in spades. I have come to recognize anxiety as the ongoing suffering of fragile X. By the time Zack was three years old, surgeries to remove his adenoids and put tubes in his ears improved his health a great deal, so he was no longer suffering physically. However, the suffering of anxiety is something that surgery cannot change. Loud, swinging fifties band music sends Zack over the edge. When a train passes by the lovely beach we enjoy, he grips my arm with terror and cries, then heads straight for the car. Crowds, sudden noises, fast cars, and too much tickling are a few of the reasons his shirts all have tiny holes chewed into them.

Tears flow instantly once Zack's threshold for stimulation has been reached. He will be laughing one minute, like he's having the best time of his life, and crying the next. Sometimes it's back and forth between laughing and crying, as he continues to demand an activity long after I know it's putting him over the edge. The return passage to a calm demeanor can seem endless.

I've heard the physiological explanations for this. The normal stress reaction that we all experience is heightened in people with fragile X, and once released into the body, the chemicals that bring on the "fight or flight" response stay elevated for many hours longer than in neurologically typical people.

Knowing this doesn't help me stop it from happening in my boy, but it does prepare me for it.

My best response to Zack's anxiety is to hold him in a swaddling embrace. A blanket helps with this, as it keeps all limbs tightly pressed to his body. I have even laid on top of him at times, and as strange as it sounds, this is very calming for my child. It is always a huge relief when his emotional equilibrium is restored.

To maintain my role as nurturer for Zack and Taylor, I fought to keep my own stress and sadness hidden—often feeling mentally like a rubber band stretched way beyond capacity. I would tighten every muscle in my body to keep from exploding.

I became angry. Angry because I didn't want to be sad anymore. Angry that my little boy had to deal with overwhelming anxiety and fragility in his emotions. Angry that he would never be able to experience life like the rest of us do. And, frankly, I was angry with God for ruining the plans I had for my life. My ideal family was a Norman Rockwell portrait. The one He had given me lacked a little girl and a fully functioning, well-connected second son.

SOCIOLOGISTS HAVE NAMED IT "UNRESOLVED GRIEF," THIS MOURNING THAT HAS NO DEFINITE BOUNDARY, THAT IS NOT ACKNOWLEDGED BY AN OFFICIAL EVENT.

I read books on grief, trying to make sense of what I was going through. One talked about the loss that families living with an Alzheimer's patient feel as they watch their loved one slip slowly away from them, until all that remains is the shell of their body. I recognized my own sadness in their stories, knowing that Zack was physically with me, yet his true self was locked away in a place that I couldn't reach.

Sociologists have named it "unresolved grief," this mourning that has no definite boundary, that is not acknowledged by an official event where loved ones gather to corporately grieve and comfort one another. There is no social protocol to follow when you're grieving because your child won't interact with the world, battles crippling anxiety, and may never develop mentally past the age of five.

EVERY DAY HELD A HUNDRED LOSSES TO MOURN.

I was ashamed, as if my sadness were a rejection of Zack, when the truth was that I felt rejected by him and like a failure as his mom. Every day held a hundred losses to mourn—the look he wouldn't return, his irritated screech when I insisted on handing him a toy, his preference for solitude that shut me out. I knew how it felt to bond with my child; Taylor and I were pros at it. The thought of never bonding with Zack was something too painful for me to accept. I somehow had to make it happen, or I wouldn't survive; I just had to figure out how.

My own constant pain and anger were hard enough to carry, but when I glimpsed sadness in Jay and Taylor, my heart tightened like a vice set to squeeze the life out of me.

As I turned off the water in the shower, I heard sobbing. I grabbed a towel and followed the sound. Rounding the kitchen's corner, I saw Taylor hunched over his cereal, tears dripping into the bowl.

"What's wrong, honey?" I whispered, dropping to my knees by his side.

"Mommy, is Zack always going to have fragile X?" he asked, his small body shaking.

"Oh, Taylor, is that what you're sad about?" I asked.

"It just seems so unfair," he replied. "It makes me so sad."

I held my child and rocked him. "I know, honey. It makes me sad too."

For February 14 we planned a special evening. Jay and Taylor helped clear the dinner dishes. I brought out the heart-shaped brownie, decorated with pink frosting and conversation hearts. Eager to celebrate at any excuse, we exchanged Valentines and dug in to the chocolate treat.

While Taylor got out the cards he'd been given by his kindergarten classmates, four-year-old Zack ran back and forth from our living room to kitchen, arms flapping and mouth frozen in position as he vocalized his new word, "Eeeeeeeeeeee." Jay tried to grab his arm and pull him to the table, but he jerked away with an annoyed squeal and continued running.

"Here, Zack. Want a brownie?" I asked hopefully. He pushed it away and continued his evening marathon.

"I FEEL SO SAD WHEN ZACK WON'T JOIN US. IT'S LIKE PART OF US IS MISSING."

With great effort, we pushed Zack's noise into the background of our minds and focused on Taylor. He eagerly held up card after card, smiling at the many expressions of friendship he'd brought home that day. We oohed and aahed as he told about the class party, our attention split between his beaming enthusiasm and Zack's frenetic racing in the adjoining room.

Full from brownies and having reached the upper limit of our tolerance for Zack's noise, Jay and I cleared the table and turned on a video. Zack was once again contained, bouncing up and down in front of his favorite movie. Taylor joined his brother, while Jay and I lingered over the dishes.

First to break the silence, Jay said, "I feel so sad when Zack won't join us. It's like part of us is missing."

I wanted to take the knife I was washing and cut out the lump swelling in my throat. I was sick and tired of hurting. Now to have my usually stoic husband express his sadness was almost too much.

I thought of the many times I had wanted Jay to share in my pain. Though never negating my feelings, every time I asked how he felt, he gave the matter of fact reply, "Honey, Zack is the way God made him. We love him, and that's all that matters." His calm acceptance of Zack's condition had made me feel alone. Why didn't he struggle with it like I did? Why wasn't he angry? Now I realized that his perspective was the ballast that kept our boat afloat.

Jay had always been there to lift me up when I needed it. Now it was my turn to offer help, but all I could manage was a muffled, "I know. I know."

"Give sorrow words: the grief that does not speak
Whispers the o'er-fraught heart and bids it break."
—WILLIAM SHAKESPEARE, *MACBETH*, ACT IV. SC. 3

"Well it is said that there is no grief like the grief which does not speak."
—HENRY W. LONGFELLOW

Each heart knows its own bitterness, and no one else can share its joy.
—PROVERBS 14:10

Chapter Seven

TURNING A CORNER
OF ACCEPTANCE

We met through a listserv on autism, Anne in Texas and me in Washington, both searching for answers. Our sons were the same age, so we shared therapy ideas and experiences. After a few weeks of corresponding, she decided to test her boy for fragile X syndrome.

She wrote, "I'll feel so guilty if I did this to my son."

My cheeks flushed at her stinging words. Zack's condition was as much a surprise to me as it was to anyone, and I wasn't sure how to swallow the heaping serving of guilt she just served me.

Soon after that, I attended a dinner put on by our church women's ministry. Nervous to be in a social situation with women I barely knew, I was glad to sit with a woman I'd been in a play group with a few years earlier. As we caught up with each other's lives, I told her about Zack. After hearing that I was a carrier of the syndrome he had, she said, "Oh, so it's your fault," and gave a short laugh.

Trained from birth to be nice at all cost, I laughed with her and said, "Exactly!" as I inwardly withdrew about a thousand miles.

Is that what everyone thinks—that it's my fault? I wondered. *It's not my fault. It's God's fault.*

I believed God was in control of all things, so it followed that He was to blame for this. The worldview that had brought me such comfort in the past now set God up as a perfect target for my rage.

But even as I blamed God, I fought feelings of guilt. I couldn't erase the words I'd heard. One day, as Jay and I went through our morning routine, I couldn't hold back any longer.

"I'm sorry…"

He looked at me with steady blue eyes. "Sorry for what, hon?" he asked.

"Sorry that I did this to you. Sorry that our son has fragile X and it's my fault," I said, my eyes burning with tears.

"Oh, honey," he replied, his eyes holding the promise of unwavering acceptance. "Please don't ever say that again. It's not your fault. It's no one's fault. Besides, you are the best thing that's ever happened in my life. I wouldn't trade you or our boys for anything."

"THERE IS NOTHING YOU COULD HAVE DONE TO PREVENT THIS. DON'T EVER FEEL GUILTY. YOU'RE NOT TO BLAME."

A couple of years later, I brought up the subject again, this time with a researcher at a fragile X conference.

"I was wondering," I began. "If I had been younger when I had my son, would there have been less of a chance that he'd have fragile X syndrome?"

"No," he said. "No, there's no correlation between a mother's age and fragile X syndrome." Then, as if sensing the true question behind my words, he said kindly, "There is nothing you could have done to prevent this. Don't ever feel guilty. You're not to blame."

The guilt for being a carrier was silenced. What remained was the guilt that said, if only I could give the missing input into Zack's life, find the silver-bullet therapy, or pray the right prayer, then he would be dramatically changed.

I had come to the weekly prayer service early. The church was dark and quiet as believers approached the altar to ask for special prayer. Our family had been here to pray for Zack before and came again tonight at the gentle urging of close friends.

PREVIOUS BLESSINGS SEEMED
LIKE DULL TRINKETS IN MY
MEMORY. I WOULD TRADE THEM
ALL FOR THIS ONE THING.

Halfway through the service, I looked up to see Jay and our two boys walking down the side aisle to meet me. Jay carried Zack, his soft golden curls silhouetted in the light from the doorway, and Taylor walked by his side, holding his free hand. My eyes filled with tears at the sight of my guys. I stepped in line, and we approached the altar together.

As Pastor Wayne prayed for Zack, I wondered how God could resist us. I couldn't have. Our faith in His goodness must move Him to heal, even if it meant a change in His original plan.

Oh, please, God, I pleaded in my heart, *please heal my baby boy.*

Days later, I continued my struggle to hear God's voice. I wanted answers. Would He heal Zack? Would He answer my prayers this time? I remembered all the times He had said yes to my requests. So many that my sister claimed I had an inside line to God's heart. Now previous blessings seemed like dull trinkets in my memory. I would trade them all for this one thing.

HOW COULD I WALK AWAY FROM MY SOURCE OF LIFE, MY ONLY TRUE HOPE? I HAD TO FOLLOW. IT WASN'T FAIR.

At dusk I heard His voice in my heart. *Will you still follow me if I don't give you what you want?*

I winced. *Do I have a choice?*

As angry as I was that God had allowed this in my life, in Zack's life, I couldn't walk away from my faith. How could I walk away from my source of life, my only true hope? I had to follow. It wasn't fair.

Will you still love me if I don't heal Zack? Will you still believe that I am good and loving and will use even this for good?

I was struggling against the inevitable. "I will try, Lord," I finally whispered. "Please help me."

I Am, was His reply.

Email became my lifeline. Jay worked long hours, and I turned to my sister Melissa, who lived three thousand miles away, for support. She held my hand across the miles as we both spent long hours alone each day, small boys swirling around our ankles, challenging our patience and emotional balance.

I poured out my hour-by-hour worries and hopes to Melissa—chronicling Zack's every move forward in development, my latest research findings on the Internet, my fury at the injustice of disability, and my deepest fears and sorrows. She received it with a calm, loving invitation to tell more. And I did.

One night, during my usual 3:00 A.M. wake up call from grief, I headed for my computer, but my lifeline was cut off. The computer wouldn't let me into my program. I rebooted and tried again. No luck. After a few more frustrated attempts, I was boiling over. That's when I got down and dirty with God.

You let my child have fragile X, and now You won't even let me write on this stupid computer! I railed. *I am so mad at You!*

I imagined the ceiling splitting open and a huge hand reaching through to slap me across the room, but I kept pouring out my fury anyway. Fists in the air, I raged, *How could you do this to me? I'm a great mother, and I should be able to have all the normal children I want. This is all your fault!*

Ten minutes later I was sobbing on the floor. I cried to exhaustion, the peace of letting my emotions go slowly replacing my anger.

BEING A FOLLOWER OF JESUS DIDN'T EXEMPT ME FROM THE PAIN AND SORROW OF THIS WORLD; IT JUST GAVE ME GRACE TO GROW IN THE MIDST OF IT.

Now that I'd gotten honest with God, I spent hours on my knees. In that place I learned that God wasn't obligated to me, that I had no predetermined right to an easy life. Gradually the question of "why me?" was replaced with "why *not* me?" Being a follower of Jesus didn't exempt me from the pain and sorrow of this world; it just gave me grace to grow in the midst of it. God didn't want to be my fairy godmother, there simply to give me what I wanted. God wanted to have a relationship with me, a real day-to-day interaction of dependence and trust. He hadn't given Zack to me carelessly. There was a purpose in who Zack was and in my being his mother. Nothing happens by accident.

I knelt at my bedside, face buried in my hands, with a picture in my mind of myself in a small cutout on the side of a sheer cliff, being held in place by God's loving hand. Day after day I came to this place, saying, *Hide me in the shadow of Your hand, Lord. Hide me under Your wing.* When nothing in my life felt secure and I couldn't trust my own emotions, I found peace in this cleft of rock. There, slowly, my fears faded away and faith took their place. We were going to be all right. That didn't mean it was going to be easy, but I knew that God was with me and I was where He wanted me to be.

There would be other dips along the way, other days when I would flop into a chair and cry out for help, days when I wanted to run away or go to sleep for a few years. But I had turned a corner of acceptance.

When we pray we must first realize that we never know better than God. The essence of prayer is not that we say to God: "Thy will be changed," but that we say to Him: "Thy will be done." So often real prayer must be, not that God would send us the things we wish, but that He would make us able to accept the things He wills.

—WILLIAM BARCLAY[1]

Be satisfied with your present circumstances and with what you have, for God Himself has said, "I will not in any way fail you nor give you up nor leave you without support. I will not, I will not, I will not in any degree leave you helpless nor forsake you nor let you down (relax My hold on you)! Assuredly not!"

—HEBREWS 13:5 (AMP)

↲ Chapter Eight

I Need Help:
Chronic Stress and Depression

Corrie and I lingered near the water's edge, throwing rocks. The inlet was quiet save for the soft plopping of pebbles and a few seals' occasional, outrageous burps. We breathed deeply, soaking the silence into our souls during this brief respite from our young sons.

"Can you remember how it felt when we were in college and could do anything we wanted with our time?" I asked.

"We didn't know how wonderful that was," she replied.

"Life was so easy then," I sighed, "and we didn't even know it."

My friend of twenty years reached over and rubbed my back. "It really stinks right now, doesn't it, sweetie?"

"Yeah, it does, and I can't do anything about it," I replied, my eyes filling with the unwelcome tears that came too easily and too often.

I looked up at the twisting madrona trees that lined the pathways leading to this cove. They held the secrets we'd shared through our adult years—the possibilities that our twenties had held, with all their turbulence and ecstasy, the joys of our engagements and weddings, the thrill and exhaustion of motherhood, the pride we felt over our excellent firstborns, and now the grief and chronic stress we lived with as we faced the challenges of our second sons, who were both on the autism spectrum. These moments together braced us for living.

"You know, no one in the Bible felt qualified to do their jobs either," Corrie said after a few minutes.

We stood and wearily walked up the path leading back to our husbands and sons.

Jay left our vacation spot later that week to return to work, but I stayed on with the boys at Corrie's family vacation getaway. I lasted three days before single parenting brought me to the breaking point. Vacation didn't exist without Jay's help, especially when I still wasn't sleeping.

"ARE YOU OKAY, MOM? I'VE NEVER SEEN YOU CRY BEFORE."

The day had started out well. Taylor was off with Tallis, his constant companion on vacation. Zack and I had gone to the beach to throw rocks and then to stretch out in the hammock to swing. As I plopped down, Corrie's twelve-year-old niece Mary came, accompanied by her golden retriever, and Zack joined them on the lawn. Mary's five-year-old twin sisters climbed onto the hammock with me. Their sweet chatter filled the air as they played with my hair.

"You have really curly hair!" they exclaimed. Their own was very straight, cut in a darling bob.

"Yes, I do," I replied. "I like yours a lot."

"Thank you. We like yours, too."

I lay there for half an hour, relaxing in the care of two little nurturers. When Zack and I returned to our cabin, I went into the bathroom, sat down, and sobbed, *God, I want a little girl. I want a little girl.*

Once the faucet was turned on, I couldn't turn it off. My body ached with longing to hold another baby.

I BREATHED A PRAYER OF THANKS THAT MY CONSTANT ATTEMPTS TO HIDE MY GRIEF WERE SUCCESSFUL, AT LEAST, IN SHELTERING TAYLOR.

Taylor came in for a snack, and I washed my face, but the tears kept coming.

"What's wrong, Mom?" he asked with alarm, wrapping his arms around me.

Unable to give him an explanation to soothe his concern, I said, "Oh, I just miss Daddy, that's all."

"I miss him too, Mom. Are you okay? I've never seen you cry before."

"I'm okay, honey. I'm just sad, that's all," I said, breathing a prayer of thanks that my constant attempts to hide my grief were successful, at least, in sheltering Taylor.

"Do you want to play a game?"

"Okay."

We played Sorry until dinner time, then walked over to join our friends. Corrie looked at my red eyes with concern.

"I saw the twins today," I said.

"They undo me too," she sighed.

We both knew the ache of that unfulfilled desire, and I was grateful for the time I'd been able to spend with my good friend, who understood me well. But after this long day, I felt drained and defeated. I knew I would return from vacation more exhausted than when we'd left.

I COULDN'T DENY THAT CHRONIC STRESS AND DEPRESSION WERE TAKING THEIR TOLL ON MY BODY AND ON MY FAMILY.

Back home I couldn't deny that chronic stress and depression were taking their toll on my body and on my family. My fight to keep frayed nerves in check each day sapped energy I needed to be a mom. I snapped at Jay often and had little patience with Taylor. The day I couldn't stop screaming at him for a minor infraction, I ran into the backyard and desperately prayed for help. I couldn't let my emotions ruin my child. Something had to be done.

A few weeks later, at my annual exam, Dr. Sim asked how it was going. "Oh, it's okay," I said, trying to sound confident.

"How are you coping with the stress in your life?" she asked.

"Well, I'm still really struggling," I admitted, "but it's so much better than it used to be. I just don't understand why I keep feeling so anxious."

"Elizabeth, how is it better than it used to be?"

"Well, Zack's older now, and when I look at my life, there just isn't as much stress as there used to be," I said weakly.

Dr. Sim smiled and said, "When I went to graduate school, I had to walk through a really rough neighborhood to get to campus. There were shootings there every week. At first my friends and I were always nervous, but after a while we got used to it and it didn't seem as bad. We had gotten used to the stress, but it was still there. Elizabeth, you have gotten used to the stress, but it's still wearing on you."

"I know," I said, my eyes filling up with tears.

"I will give you something to help, if you ever want it," she said.

I had been praying for peace for a long time. My sister and friends kept suggesting that I try an antidepressant. I had debated with myself for two years now, and I wondered if maybe this was an answer to my prayers after all. It certainly would be a relief to be free of this debilitating anxiety. Toughing it out on my own wasn't working.

Just as she was opening the door to leave the room, I said, "I think I would like to try something."

"I think that would be a good idea," Dr. Sim replied as she turned back around and wrote a prescription.

That night I took a pill and drifted off to sleep. When I woke up the next morning, I couldn't believe I had slept all night. Within days I felt better. In a few weeks I had a sense of well-being that I hadn't had for years. The medication didn't make life blissful, but it took the edge off my anxiety, which enabled me to cope with my life again. I was able to remember things, I could focus on one thought without obsessing about other things, and I had energy to play with my boys again. With gratefulness I recognized how good and necessary accepting help was for me and for my family.

I learned for myself that the path out of the valley of depression is slow and laborious. From the time of my first panic attack in 1990, it took me over five years to recover, and I can't tell how long I was depressed before I had to face up to it and find help. Many times, storm clouds rolled over the mountains and drenched me in showers of tears. Many times, I almost missed the beams of hope gleaming through the black clouds.

But in the mountains, after the storms pass, the air is fresh, the sky, a clean translucent blue. Wildflowers that were watered by the rains paint the fields with brilliant colors as far as the eye can see. Like Solomon, I can say, "See! The winter is past; the rains are over. Flowers appear on the earth; the season of singing has come."

That is what I see in my life now: a fresh newness, a spring-like beauty and joy. Through the valleys of depression and the storms of tears, the promises of God have proven true in my life.

—JAN DRAVECKY[1]

Even when we are too weak to have any faith left, he remains faithful to us and will help us, for he cannot disown us who are part of himself, and he will always carry out his promises to us.

—2 TIMOTHY 2:13 (TLB)

Chapter Nine

OVERCOMING
BITTERNESS AND SELF–PITY

When I was a little girl, my father used to say to me, "Elizabeth, you have a lot of love inside of you to give." I'm always high on the mercy scale when I take those tests that show what kind of a person you are. You know, the type who cringes during Marx Brothers movies while everyone else is howling with laughter and cries when an Olympic skater falls. I always root for the underdog.

With this seemingly innate compassion, you would think that living with grief would have made me even more merciful toward others. Eventually it did, but first I had to deal with the self-pity and bitterness in my own heart.

Bitterness makes everyone else's pain seem trivial. It locks us in a closet of self-pity that leads to self-absorption and blindness to the needs around us. When we're bitter, we don't see the pain of others, and we don't care about it anyway.

All I cared about was having my own pain go away. I just wanted it to be over with, to get on with life and be happy again. But it wasn't that simple. My grieving was endlessly cyclical.

Each cycle was less intense, but my dips into sadness and fear kept happening long after my rational mind was ready for me to dust myself off and be on my way. And every time I felt myself sinking into the sadness again, I wanted to punch a hole in the wall. It was easier to be angry than crumble into tears.

BITTERNESS FILLED MY FIELD OF VISION EVEN THOUGH I DIDN'T SEE IT.

Just when I would start to feel like I had a handle on things emotionally, it would be time for another yearly evaluation for my little boy. The inevitable heartache that each review brought sent me into a tailspin, no matter how hard I fought against the downward spiral.

One of the worst of these evaluations was the IQ test that came when Zack turned six. The school psychologist arrived on time, suggesting we sit on the floor so Zack would feel comfortable. I agreed.

I knew Zack wouldn't perform well on the tests. He never did. Still, they had to be done for school-funding reasons, so we complied. I had been trying to prepare for weeks, mentally coaching myself that the results didn't change anything, that he was still Zack and that the numbers didn't matter.

Dr. Rich took out ten tests designed to rate the ability of three- to six-year-olds to respond to new situations and simple tasks. He set out a puzzle with three rectangles of varying sizes. Zack easily put them in their correct places, and we cheered. He smiled proudly.

Next the doctor put out a puzzle of a flower. Zack tried repeatedly to put a petal in upside-down. *Not a big deal*, I thought. *At least he knows where it goes.* With a little help, he finished the puzzle. Cheers again and another broad smile.

Test number three involved choosing the matching figure from a field of three choices. "Point to same," I said. Zack put his small index finger on the matching choice, and we cheered. Same task, again with success and more cheers. Next page, same task, but this time he pointed to all three choices and repeated, "Same," wearing a cheerful grin as if to say, "I have this game down pat."

On the fourth test Zack had to choose the biggest bunny on the page. Again he pointed cheerfully to each bunny and said, "Same."

How can someone fail at something they have no control over? I argued, trying to talk sense to my emotions.

My heart beat faster as my mind obsessed. *It's absurd to teach a child those concepts when he's still working on basic words like eat and* drink, I assured myself. *Yes, but what kind of a mother doesn't teach* biggest *and* smallest? my mind screamed back. The blood pounded between my ears, beating out a pattern of *failure, Failure, FAILURE!*

And all the while, my sunny little boy kept pointing to the pictures on each test and saying, "Same. Same. Same." As each box was returned to its place, Dr. Rich and I told Zack what a good job he was doing and he smiled ever more broadly, sure of his success and confident of his worth.

Weeks later the results were in and we were given an IQ score so low it hurts too much to write it down. *It's just a number*, I said to myself, *just a number*, once again hearing the judgment of "failure as a mom" in the court of my mind. *How can someone fail at something they have no control over?* I argued, trying to talk sense to my emotions. *God made him who he is, and I can't change that. My job is just to love him.*

"It's just a number after all," I said out loud as Zack beamed in my direction.

Just a number and another label that will fade in time, allowing me to see my little boy once again, but right then it still hurt, and bitterness filled my field of vision even though I didn't see it.

Soon after this evaluation, my sister emailed me about her oldest son's struggles in school. Although he was an early reader and quite verbal, math didn't come easily for him, and other tasks caused such frustration that he frequently flew into rages. The teacher recommended he repeat kindergarten.

I read her emails and thought, *At least he can talk! At least he looks you in the eye! He's potty-trained! What have you got to complain about? Repeating kindergarten is okay. He's going to grow up and be a functioning adult!*

NO ONE HAD AS BIG A PROBLEM OR AS MUCH OF A REASON TO BE SAD AS I DID.

I'd thrown compassion out the window. No one had as big a problem or as much of a reason to be sad as I did. My rut of self-pity and bitterness was deep and wide, and I had no idea I was even in it.

I emailed back to Melissa. In my heart I knew my words were insensitive, if not hurtful, as I pointed out that she had a lot to be grateful for and that repeating a grade wasn't that big of a deal, but I ignored the inner warning. A day later I received her angry reply.

She said, "Of all people, I thought that you would understand what it feels like to worry about your child." She ended her email with the following quote from Holocaust survivor Viktor Frankl:

> A man's suffering is similar to the behavior of gas. If a certain quantity of gas is pumped into an empty chamber, it will fill the chamber. Thus suffering completely fills the human soul and conscious mind, no matter whether the suffering is great or little. Therefore the "size" of human suffering is absolutely relative.[1]

Melissa's pain and sense of betrayal was a mirror held up, and I finally saw the bitterness in my heart. The cruelty of its fruit expressed toward one who had been my constant support made me sick to my stomach.

Shaking, I got down on my knees. "Oh God, forgive me," I cried. "Forgive me for continuing to resent what You've given me. Forgive me for being bitter toward You for letting Zack have fragile X. Forgive me, and help Melissa to forgive me too."

Then I wrote and asked Melissa to forgive me.

She did.

As I looked hard into the mirror that this incident with my sister held up to my heart, I found inspiration in the insight of Mother Teresa, who knew suffering very well. She expressed my experience when she said:

> We must have the courage to pray to have the courage to accept. Because we do not pray enough, we see only the human part. We don't see the divine. And we resent it. I think that much of the misunderstanding of suffering today comes from that, from resentment and bitterness. Bitterness is an infectious disease, a cancer, an anger hidden inside.[2]

When I realized the hidden trap of bitterness and self-pity I had been in, I was able once again to see past my own situation and into the lives of other people. Now, rather than being blind to the pain of others, it is a relief to be able to reach out to them in mercy, extending the understanding I have so desperately needed myself.

♪ *I have learned from experience that the greater part of our happiness or misery depends on our disposition and not on our circumstances.*

—MARTHA WASHINGTON[3]

♪ *Self-pity is our worst enemy and if we yield to it, we can never do anything wise in the world.*

—HELEN KELLER

♪ *A repining life is a lingering death.*

—BENJAMIN WHICHCOTE (1610–1683)

♪ *See to it that no one misses the grace of God and that no bitter root grows up to cause trouble and defile many.*

—HEBREWS 12:15

Chapter Ten

IN THE COMMUNITY: TRUSTING THE KINDNESS OF OTHERS

*T*he director of the children's ministry at our church poked her head in the door of the class my husband was teaching and scanned the room with a tentative smile. Seeing me, she beckoned with her finger apologetically. I reached for the diaper in my purse and got up to follow her, as she quietly shut the door. When she opened it again, I saw the look of urgency on her face and knew this wasn't an ordinary diaper call.

"Did Zack strip in the classroom?" I asked, as I joined Allison in the hallway. We sped around the corner to the kindergarten room, and she giggled, "Poor Amber just isn't sure how to deal with that."

We entered the room to find an orderly group of three- to five-year-olds eating their snack at one end of the room, while Amber stood over Zack at the other. My five-year-old was naked from the waist down, flailing his legs so that she couldn't put his pants back on.

In my firmest voice, I said, "Zack, you keep your clothes on in public," pinned his legs down, and dressed him.

Though I had warned the childcare providers of Zack's latest behavior when I dropped him off that night, they had underestimated his speed and agility when it came to stripping his clothes off and gleefully running around in the buff. I could picture the scene as Amber exclaimed, "He's so feisty!" Her flushed face showed the effort it had taken to catch him. The other children looked on momentarily, lost interest, and resumed their snacking. Thank goodness they hadn't followed suit.

MY OWN INSECURITY KEPT ME ON THE LOOKOUT FOR ANY SIGN OF REJECTION.

We had a good laugh, and I left to rejoin my group. When I picked Zack up twenty minutes later, he ran to me, beaming with the sweetness of an angel.

Though I laugh often with our church childcare workers over Zack's antics, I struggled at first not to second-guess their reactions. My own insecurity kept me on the lookout for any sign of rejection.

I saw them exchange glances as we walked in the door. Resisting the urge to grab Zack's hand and run out of the building, I picked up the pen and signed my name to the child register instead. Then I kissed Zack goodbye and crossed the hallway to my Friday-night Bible study.

I could hear Zack's moans as the teenage helpers walked him up and down the hall, trying to keep him entertained while the other children played games and participated in crafts. Straining to pick up any intonation of impatience in the voices across the hall, I heard none, so I returned my attention to the teaching on the book of James.

But I couldn't keep my mind focused and took up my usual Friday night lament instead. *Lord, should I even be in this class?*

Maybe I should just stay home on Fridays. I hate to bother these girls with a child who doesn't go along with the group. It's so humiliating to have a child who needs extra help. I feel like a burden!

"I HAVE BEEN TOTALLY BLESSED BY YOUR SON THIS QUARTER. HE IS SO SWEET. AND I HAVE SO MUCH ADMIRATION FOR YOU."

During the next ten weeks of the study, I was able to relax more about Zack's situation and actually absorb some teaching. Still, I was relieved to pick him up for the final time.

As Zack and I turned to leave the playroom, Sharon, one of the helpers, stopped me. "I just wanted to tell you that I have been totally blessed by your son this quarter. He is so sweet. And I have so much admiration for you."

I was stunned. "Thank you for telling me that," I stammered.

I left with a prayer on my heart. *Lord, help me stop assuming what others are thinking. Help me trust them and believe the best about them.*

It's a lesson I've learned many times since Zack was born.

My family is incredibly blessed to worship in a church where Zack is accepted and loved. Our other communities are the same way, although each situation poses a challenge initially before we break through the acquaintance barrier and become friends and as we ourselves work out the best way to help Zack participate.

Some of the first sporting events at Taylor's school, in particular, were quite tense for me before I came to the conclusion that I didn't have to include Zack in every family activity.

Taylor dribbled the basketball down the court and took a shot. I yelled, "Yay!" as the ball swooshed through the hoop—

and simultaneously raced toward the court to grab Zack and keep him from being trampled in the game he was so eager to join. He fought to get free as I pulled him back to the sidelines.

I HAD BECOME SO USED TO STRUGGLING THAT IT WAS A RELIEF TO REALIZE THAT NOT EVERY FIGHT HAD TO BE FACED HEAD-ON.

By halftime I was dripping with sweat, my arms and back ached, and I had bruises on my shins from Zack's enthusiastic kicking. Keeping him out of the game gave me more of a work-out than the boys on the court were getting, and I was thankful for the break in action.

Zack gleefully ran around the court with other younger siblings while coaches huddled with their respective teams, strategizing for the second half of the game. First-grade basketball was serious stuff. I caught my breath and relaxed for a few minutes.

When the whistle blew, I was on duty again. I ran to get Zack, who dramatically flung himself onto the court and refused to move. When I reached for him, he kicked and twisted out of the way.

Parents stared and little boys got into position to begin the third quarter. Mustering all my strength to take control over this fifty-pound muscleboy, I picked Zack up and half carried, half dragged him off the court while he pulled my hair with both his hands and all his strength.

As my face flushed hotter than an outside heating lamp, I plopped down on a shaky folding chair and vowed, "Never again. Not without Jay."

I had become so used to struggling that it was a relief to real-ize that not every fight had to be faced head-on. In time we took advantage of other, more suitable opportunities for Zack to make friends with people in Taylor's school community.

Long before we got into any social situations, I worried myself sick about how children would respond to Zack. I figured I could count on adults to be kind, but I wasn't one bit sure about children. My mind played out horrible scenarios that made my mother-bear persona stand up to full height. I would sit at McDonald's tense and ready for a fight with the first two-year-old to poke fun at my baby.

One time, two little boys weren't letting Zack get into the restaurant's play structure with them. He was making really loud noises, and they were staring at him with nervous looks on their faces. I explained in simple terms that Zack can't talk, but he can hear everything they say, and that he makes funny noises, but he feels just like they do. Then, to my amazement, they let him in.

I WASN'T ABOUT TO ENTRUST MY SWEET SON TO THE MERCY OF OTHERS.

I once heard a conference speaker say that parents of special-needs children need to trust other kids to be kind. If we don't, we overprotect and our child doesn't have the opportunity to interact with the world. I listened to that speaker and thought, "Nice theory, but no way! I'm not throwing my child to the wolves. Absolutely not!" I wasn't about to entrust my sweet son to the mercy of others. Since then I have been forced to take baby steps in this direction, and the more I risk it, the easier it becomes.

Everywhere we go, kids are always trying to figure Zack out. They watch him quizzically at first. The younger ones might poke or prod him to get a response. Sometimes the very young don't notice that he isn't talking back and just count him as one of their friends, but it isn't long before most of them know that something is different about him. However, their response is far more accepting than I expected.

Taylor and his cousin Quinn were playing a video game. Zack sat next to them, handling the controls of their extra equipment.

QUINN: He's pretty smart.
TAYLOR: Yeah.
QUINN: He can pretty much do anything anyone else can do, except talk.
TAYLOR: Yeah.
QUINN: He's just like us, he just doesn't talk.
TAYLOR: Yeah.
QUINN: So he's a smart fellow, he just doesn't talk.
TAYLOR: Yeah.

    Pause.

TAYLOR: Sometimes he talks.
QUINN: If you tell him something to say, will he say it?
TAYLOR: Sometimes.

Then Taylor leaned over to Zack and said, "One. One. One."

QUINN: What are you trying to get him to say?
TAYLOR: Well, sometimes he counts.

After many experiences of acceptance and kindness, and as our network of supportive family, friends, and acquaintances has grown, I have learned to relax about Zack's idiosyncratic behavior. I used to break out in cold sweats and feel lightheaded at the attention his noise and actions brought our way. Then I realized that fainting, or death, would leave my children stranded in whatever public place we happened to be in at the time, so I had

I TOLD MYSELF THAT WHATEVER PEOPLE
WERE THINKING, THEY WERE PROBABLY
WRONG—ZACK WASN'T A SPOILED BRAT,
HE WAS AUTISTIC; AND I WASN'T AN
IDIOT, I WAS A GOOD MOTHER.

to learn how to keep my heart rate down. To do this, I forced my mind to focus on meeting Zack's needs and block out everything else. I repeatedly told myself that whatever people were thinking, they were probably wrong—Zack wasn't a spoiled brat, he was autistic; and I wasn't an idiot, I was a good mother. As time went on and I became more comfortable with my son, I was able to relax and see the humor in some situations.

I remember one day in particular when I pushed Zack around in the grocery cart as he yelled his usual, over-the-top grocery-store noises. He sat facing me, arms and feet flailing, as I bent over to avoid being kicked. I sang songs and made animal noises in an attempt to entertain him, not caring that everyone knew we were coming!

A friendly woman approached us at the seafood department. As her cart rolled next to ours, I stopped to get an eyelash out of my eye. The woman began to ask me about Zack, and I explained that he has fragile X syndrome, as I maneuvered my contact lens to get the eyelash out from under it.

"Oh, dear, is this hard for you to talk about?" she asked me, mistaking the stream of tears on my face for sadness.

"Oh, no," I said, "I just have something in my eye."

"Oh. Well, he's going to be all right you know," she assured me. "One day he'll be living on his own."

"Actually, probably not," I said, now trying to move my contact back into place, my head down and eyes still streaming.

"Well, at least he'll be able to take care of himself for the most part," she continued.

I wanted to let her off the hook and continue my shopping, but I felt compelled to be completely honest in those days, so I replied, "Well, there's no guarantee of that really."

"Well, at least he'll be able to talk," she concluded triumphantly.

"We'll see," I said. "Right now we're not sure about that either." By now, my tears were a smothered urge to laugh. This nice lady was so earnest in her search for something comforting to say, and she was batting a big zero.

Unable to think of anything more to say, she said, "Well, he's alive at least!"

"Yes, he is. And we love him!" I exclaimed with gusto, and breathing a sigh of relief, I pushed our cart toward Dairy.

I have outgrown my urge to tell our entire story to complete strangers, but the teacher in me still sees questions as an opportunity to educate. In addition to wanting people to be informed, I've found that playing the role of teacher removes me from the emotion of the message, a distance I welcome at times. Sometimes, though, I am caught off guard and have no response but the raw truth. Such was the case with a group of new friends from Taylor's school.

It was a perfect August day when the boys and I met some fellow first-grade families to play at a park. I sat with the moms, angling myself so I could keep my eyes on Zack as he headed off to a remote picnic table and still join in the conversation. While Taylor ran around and splashed in the water with his friends, Zack sat on the table he had chosen in the shade, rocking and chewing his shirt. He returned occasionally to make what I call "fly-by" contact with the group, but he always retreated again to his seclusion.

Enter Lijah, the cheerful one-year-old brother of Taylor's friend Logan. He crawled over and gleefully plunked himself down amidst the water spouts, gurgling as his Michelin-tire-shaped arms and legs were cooled by the misty spray.

On Zack's next fly-by, he noticed Lijah. Just as he does with our cats at home and with every dog at the park, Zack bent over to smile at Lijah warmly. As Lijah moved between the safety of his mom and the thrill of water, Zack followed him.

"FOR I KNOW THE PLANS I HAVE FOR ZACK, PLANS TO PROSPER HIM AND NOT TO HARM HIM. PLANS TO GIVE HIM A FUTURE AND A HOPE."

Lijah's mom, Rhonda, said cheerfully, "Oh, look at Zack with Lijah. He really likes babies. Don't you ever just look at him and wonder what his future will be like?"

Blurting out the first thought that came to mind, I admitted, "I try not to think of the future because, to be honest, it always makes me despair."

Instantly I felt guilty over those horrible words and wondered if I had shocked these supermoms. Yet how could I possibly feel positive about Zack's future when I was so afraid of it? I had talked to a lot of people about Zack, but no one had ever indicated that they expected his future to be positive. No one asked questions as if they thought of him as a real person.

Yet, here was this upbeat mom asking me about Zack's future, as if she totally expected me to have dreams and visions for him like I did for Taylor. It rattled me.

But it didn't rattle these women. In chorus they claimed Jeremiah 29:11 for me, and for Zack: "For I know the plans I have for Zack, plans to prosper him and not to harm him. Plans to give him a future and a hope."

It was an instance of recognition: I was with sisters, partners in motherhood and in this walk of faith. I was not alone.

I didn't leave the play date bubbling over, but I did leave feeling understood. My new friends hadn't deluged me with false promises or unrealistic hope. They saw my reality and didn't try to speak it away. Yet they turned me to the truth of God's Word and reminded me that He holds the future and I can hope in Him.

Never bend your head. Always hold it high. Look the world straight in the face.

—Helen Keller

Love bears up under anything and everything that comes, is ever ready to believe the best of every person, its hopes are fadeless under all circumstances, and it endures everything without weakening.

—1 Corinthians 13:7 (AMP)

SMALL MIRACLES: CONNECTING WITH WORDS AND GAMES

*B*efore Zack was born, reading books and playing games together was a constant part of the days I spent with Taylor, and those activities still continue for us. But for so long, communicating with Zack through playful interactions and language was only a dream. Because of this, every initial connection Zack and I made, every milestone he achieved, is framed in my memory as the small miracle it was.

Sometime during his fourth year, on one of our weekly Wednesday nights alone, Zack sat on my knees as we played on my bed. He leaned close to my face as I sang one of his favorite songs, "The Wheels on the Bus." At the end of each verse, I dropped my knees and he fell backwards with a delighted giggle.

After a dozen rounds of the song, Zack and I were both laughing. Through his giggles, he hummed "m…m, m, m, m, mmmmmmmm" to a melody. I repeated it, much to his glee. We took turns, changing the melody slightly each time. The door had opened for a wordless language between us. From then on, whenever he was unhappy, I would "m, m, m, m, m, mmmmm-mmmm" and he would laugh and hum back.

I HAD SO OFTEN WONDERED IF HE REALLY SAW ME, IF I REALLY WAS A PART OF HIS WORLD.

About this time, I decided to assume Zack was watching me peripherally, even when he wouldn't look at my eyes. I also began talking to him like he understood, whether or not he gave any indication of it. It soon became obvious that he did understand most of what I said. His smiles at my antics and the way he followed directions encouraged me to keep pursuing this little boy so locked within himself.

It was during that year that Zack and I played our very first verbal game together, that glorious day as I pushed him in his swing and he surprised me with a new word, "Boo!" As I wrote in the preface, without thinking I answered, "Don't you say 'boo,' or I'll have to tickle you!"—and to my amazement and delight Zack laughed and said, "Boo!" He did understand—and he had a sense of humor too.

Then one day, when he was five, Zack pulled his shirt up over his face and giggled.

"Where's Zack?" I singsonged.

Quickly pulling his shirt down, he replied, "Boo boo, I see lu!"

It was his first complete sentence, and it answered my heart's cry better than any other words could have. He saw me! I had so often wondered if he really saw me, if I really was a part of his world. Now I knew. He had said the words himself. He saw me.

The words were beginning to come after three years of intense therapy. To me it was a bonus, as I had all but given up hope that Zack would ever talk. His words were only close approximations, but the intonation was there and, just as a toddler's parents know what he or she is saying long before anyone else does, we understood Zack's language and applauded it with great delight

Zack was also taking delight in his new language skills.

I sat typing emails at my computer one afternoon while Zack bounced on the bed behind me. He was ready to play so he came and pulled me over, something he had only recently begun to do. Covering his head with my comforter, he intoned, "Where go?" in a squeaky voice filled with laughter.

Forcing myself to leave my adult world for the moment, I joined in our now three-month-long game of peekaboo. "Where did Zack go?"

More laughter came from under the covers.

"Where did he go?" I repeated, my voice rising higher and higher.

Suddenly Zack threw the covers off, revealing his beaming face. "Keep poo, ah see lu!" he said.

At least twenty-five rounds later, he continued repeating the words while I now lay next to him, interspersing tickling and other brief games with his favorite one.

Pausing for a moment, he turned to me and smacked his lips several times. Then, in his lowest growl of a voice, he said, "Saaaaaaaaaaaaaaaaaaaaaaaaaay."

I laughed, recognizing the line from his favorite book, and continued it for him. "I like green eggs and ham. I do. I like them, Sam I am!"

We both giggled with joy! It was Zack's first joke.

Zack's vocabulary was growing, but that didn't mean we were *always* able to understand his words.

"I-nu-tie! I-nu-tie! I-nu-tie!" my cheerful little rooster crows at 4:00 A.M.

Through dream-filled thoughts, I try to decipher Zack's announcement of vital importance, knowing he is strutting about the house gathering his icons and building his altars—a photo of Taylor's baseball team propped beside his CD player, three red blocks stacked on top of each other, five precisely half-filled water glasses arranged in a semi-circle, and his treasured bowl of crackers. Once the necessary items are in place, Zack blares his tunes, singing along to "The Wheels on the Bus," "Down on Grampa's Farm," and other preschool favorites.

On days where kindness prevails, Zack sleeps until 5:30 or even 6:00. The "I-nu-tie!" chant continues until replaced with familiar songs blaring from music boxes throughout the house. As Zack turns on one piece of electronic equipment after another, my mind continues to probe the significance of this new word—*i-nu-tie*.

"Did you hear Zack's word again this morning?" I ask at breakfast, setting Jay and Taylor to the work of decoding. None of us had a clue.

Weeks later my mind heard clearly, in that place between deep sleep and wide awake, "I'm not tired! I'm not tired! I'm not tired!"

"Aha! You're not tired! But the rest of us are. Now, Zack, pleeeeeeease…go back to bed!"

One day Zack and I went on an errand to a bookstore. I tried to keep him close as I talked with the woman behind the counter, but he wandered off. Keeping an eye out for the general direction he was headed, I finished my business and followed him.

He had made his way to the children's section and was perusing his favorite books. I stood back and watched. His search was purposeful, not just a random pulling of books off the shelves. He went right to a large board-book copy of *Goodnight Moon* and sat down to read it. It is one his therapist Heidi kept in her box and took away with her after their sessions.

I listened as my son recited lines from the book. Tears welled up in my eyes, and I longed for a tape recorder to capture his voice as it rose and fell in rhythm.

"N grt grnnnn roommmmmmm, bahloonnnnnnnn, mooooooooooo, cow, moonnnnnnnnnnnnnn, ittle bears, ittle kittnnnnnnnns, pair of mttnsssssss."

We bought the largest copy they had.

"The greatest gift we can give to one another is rapt attention to one another's existence."

—SUE ATCHLEY EBAUGH

And God is able to make all grace abound to you, so that in all things at all times, having all that you need, you will abound in every good work.

—2 CORINTHIANS 9:8

⸝ Chapter Twelve

READY TO TACKLE
THE NEXT THING

Ouch! Zachary!" Taylor screamed and burst into tears. "Mom, Zachary bit me!"

I turned to look back from the passenger side of the front seat and answered, "Oh, honey, I'm sorry. Are you all right?"

"No," Taylor continued to cry, "he just reached over and bit me for no reason."

"Honey, I'm sorry, but you know Zachary doesn't understand."

"He does too understand. He never gets in trouble, Mom, and I always do. It's not my fault, but you always say it is!" Taylor's voice escalated with anger that had been brewing for months. "He's just a spoiled brat, Mom."

"Taylor, don't talk about your brother that way," I replied, casting a look that begged for help from Jay in the driver's seat.

"Taylor," Jay began, "I know that Zack does things you don't like sometimes, but he just doesn't understand not to do them. We have to teach him not to bite."

"But you let him do it! You never make him say he's sorry or anything," Taylor countered.

"Taylor, Zack can't talk. How's he going to say he's sorry?" I asked.

We drove the last few blocks to our home in silence with Taylor sulking in the backseat.

WHENEVER ZACK DID *ANYTHING*, WE WERE EXHILARATED. WE DIDN'T CARE IF IT WAS NAUGHTY, WE WERE JUST THRILLED HE HAD TAKEN INITIATIVE.

After the boys were in bed that night, Jay and I returned to the subject. "He's right, you know," Jay said. "Zachary never has any consequences to his behavior. I don't blame Taylor for being mad."

"I know," I agreed. "But what can we do? Zack cries when we say the word *naughty*."

"Well, we have to say *something* to him when he kicks or bites. We can't let him get away with this."

"It's only going to get worse if we don't do something," I agreed. "I'm worried Taylor will start hating Zack if we let this continue."

So we decided that although Zack probably wouldn't understand, we would reprimand him when he behaved inappropriately. For Taylor's sake.

Our first opportunity came the next day. We had just turned the corner on our way to the grocery store when Taylor yelped, "Ouch! Mom, Zachary kicked me."

"Zachary," I said in a firm voice as I looked in the rearview mirror, "*Do not* kick Taylor. That was naughty."

As I expected, Zack's face crumpled and he immediately burst into tears. I reached back and rubbed his leg. "Honey, it's all right. Mommy isn't mad at you. But you must not kick Taylor. No kicking."

"Yeah," Taylor echoed. "No kicking!"

Zack began pulling on his own hair and screaming, "No, no!"

"That's enough, Taylor," I said. "I'll do the disciplining here."

We read that a child with special needs must be treated as much like a typically developing child as possible. Special needs shouldn't exempt them from a basic code of conduct.

It was true, of course. However, my mother's heart majors on mercy and has a hard time disciplining at all, much less when it concerns my angel-faced, fragile son. And I think Jay would admit to being just as reluctant to call Zack on things as I am.

For one thing, it took years before Zack *did* anything naughty. In fact, for the first few years of his life he wasn't doing much of anything at all. Whenever he did *anything*, we were exhilarated. We didn't care if it was naughty, we were just thrilled he had taken initiative and acted on something!

AS WITH MOST THINGS, DISCIPLINE HAS BEEN A MATTER OF MY READINESS TO TACKLE THE ISSUE, RATHER THAN ZACK'S.

If not for Taylor, we might still be allowing Zack to do whatever he wanted. But we couldn't get away with the double standard for long, and so we began to reign Zack in. Much to our surprise, Zack's behavior changed almost immediately. Imagine that! He really seemed to know what was right and wrong, or maybe he just really needed our approval. Whichever it was, car rides are much more pleasant now that he doesn't bite and kick Taylor anymore. More important, Taylor no longer feels singled out and resentful.

As with most things, discipline has been a matter of my readiness to tackle the issue, rather than Zack's. His habits of pottying, eating, sleeping, and socializing have all required focused training. When I decided it was time for Zack to do something new, often something I had wanted for years but didn't think possible, I would figure out how to do it with him and he would follow my lead. It seems like a no-brainer for a mom to realize this, but it was part of my mind-set of parenting a special-needs child that needed to be adjusted.

Zack was six years and four months old and only partially potty-trained. He loved to stand and imitate his father and brother at the toilet but refused to sit down on it. Each time I changed a diaper, I prayed, *Father, please help Zack get potty-trained. Please don't make me change his diaper when he's a teenager.* I wished desperately that someone else would potty-train this child! I had no idea how to begin.

I WISHED DESPERATELY THAT SOMEONE ELSE WOULD POTTY–TRAIN THIS CHILD! I HAD NO IDEA HOW TO BEGIN.

I don't know how I decided that Thursday was the day, but I'm sure Zack's teacher had something to do with it. We both had been waiting for him to be potty-ready, and that day we agreed he was. When we discussed it before school, Norma said, "Maybe you're just going to have to hold him on the toilet and make him go."

As my unsuspecting child got off the bus that day, I was ready. He made his usual beeline for the closet to get a Pull-Up, and I followed. Putting them out of reach, I signed and said, "Zack, all gone. No more Pull-Ups. It's time to poop on the toilet like a big boy."

His body twisted away from me as he let out an annoyed squeal. "Come on, sweetie. Come to the toilet with Mommy," I beckoned, holding up a new game called Baby, one of his favorites at school. He followed the game into the bathroom. I picked him up, set him on the toilet, and let him play with the game for a minute. Then I took it away and said, "You can play Baby after you poop in the toilet."

My usually compliant six-year-old spent the next two-and-a-half hours rolling on the floor, searching for Pull-Ups, chewing me out in his own garbled language, and crying. Whenever he stopped fighting long enough to wince with the need to poop, I firmly placed him back on the toilet seat. Then I sat in front of him, his feet on my knees, reading and singing to him. He often flopped over and let me rub his back, our faces cheek to cheek, as I whispered, "You're doing great, sweetie. You can do it."

I CHEERED FOR HIM, FOR US. WE HAD OUR FIRST VICTORY. WE WERE ON OUR WAY!

After four hours he couldn't hold it any longer. A look of terror flashed across his face, and he fiercely grabbed my arm. The deed was quickly done and in the toilet. I cheered for him, for us. We had our first victory. We were on our way!

Next day, same scene. Same success. I canceled plans for the weekend so that we could keep our focus. Zack and I were running a race here, and I was determined to get us across the finish line.

We spent the weekend in a huddle of two. In between trips to the toilet, we hung out in Zack's room singing songs, reading books, playing peekaboo. He learned independence, and I learned perseverance, along with dozens of songs and games. There was a sweetness in this joint effort, now that we were working toward a common goal.

Monday morning I called Zack's school to report our progress, and they agreed to keep up the work. On the sixth day, I rounded the corner of our bathroom door and saw Zack proudly sitting on the toilet by himself. We were crossing the finish line. The crowd began to cheer and confetti flew through the air. I contemplated sending Pull-Ups to everyone we knew, with "WE DID IT!" written in permanent marker.

I HAD CROSSED A BARRIER OF SELF–DOUBT ERECTED YEARS BEFORE.

My heart swelled with pride over this milestone, and Zack was thrilled with himself. We had run a marathon together. "There is nothing we can't do now!" I crowed with delight, knowing I had also crossed a barrier of self-doubt erected years before.

The next day Zack practiced for hours, sitting, wiping, and flushing. I cut him off after three rolls.

The year Zack got potty-trained was a great school year for him. He was in a combined kindergarten through second-grade class, he had a wonderful teacher, and we had seen much progress. He often approached us to play, he began to notice and interact with his peers, and he understood and followed commands. At school he participated in all of the activities and was able to do independent tasks with support for up to twenty-five minutes.

I was excited to meet with his teacher, Norma, for the annual review, sure that it would be fun to review my boy's growth together.

The first item on the page was a developmental assessment of Zack, based on a standardized scale. It read:

Gross Motor	2.0 years
Fine Motor	1.0 years
Self Help	2.5 years
General Knowledge and Comprehension	1.6 years
Social and Emotional	1.0 years

I felt the familiar churning in my stomach and dryness in my mouth as my mind raced: *But he throws his own garbage away now. He's potty-trained! He understands everything we tell him to do. I know he does. He's made so much progress! How can we still be here on the scale?* And, of course, the recurring, *I'm not doing enough! If only I spent more time…*

"ALL I KNOW TO DO
IS THE NEXT THING."

We reviewed next year's goals before Norma said, "You seem upset. Is something bothering you?"

"It makes me so sad to see these numbers," I replied. "When I'm with Zack, he's just Zack. But then I see these numbers, and I just hate them!"

"I know," she said, "and they're just numbers, Elizabeth. The low scores are mostly because he doesn't talk. I hate to even write them, but I have to."

She understood. She loved my boy and wished she could make it all better. She herself had faced the challenges of parenting a child with extra needs.

And then she said a very wise thing. She said, "All I know to do is the next thing."

The "next thing" was the food issue. I knew it would be the hardest thing we'd done yet because Zack had always called the shots about what he ate. It's hard to force a child to eat something that he later throws up. And Zack threw up every day, often many times. Any kind of animal protein made him gag. The same was true with vegetables and fruit. The only thing he seemed able to eat was crackers and chips. We felt horribly guilty about this and knew it needed to change, but we couldn't make him eat better food, so we supplemented his milk with protein powder and gave him chewy vitamins.

THE OTHER CHILDREN IN HIS CLASS WITH THE SAME DISABILITY WERE EATING RICE AND VEGETABLES FOR LUNCH, AND ZACK'S DIET NEEDED TO CHANGE.

It took me ten months to get up the courage to tackle this next milestone. Zack's teacher and I talked about it during his fall conference. The other children in his class with the same disability were eating rice and vegetables for lunch, and Zack's diet needed to change.

"Just tell me what to do, Norma," I said.

"We use these cards at school all the time," she assured me as she whipped out a laminated card with "First" and "Then" printed on it. Next to each word was a Velcro strip. Once we decided what we wanted Zack to eat, we would put a picture of it next to the "First" sign. He would have to take one bite of that food, chew it, and swallow. Then he would get a bite of something he really liked for the "Then" choice as his reward.

It sounded simple, but we both knew it was going to be excruciating for a few days.

"Now, when I did this with my son," Norma warned, "he starved himself for three days. But then he ate."

"Great," I winced, knowing my little angel boy had a will of steel and could easily hold out that long.

Monday morning rolled around all too quickly, and Zack woke up to a different world. The pantry he'd had full access to before was locked and the refrigerator had a bungee cord wrapped around it. Whining, he came to my bedside and pulled at my hand.

"Hi, Zack," I said, feigning cheerfulness. "Are you hungry? Mommy will get some breakfast for you."

I let him pull me to the kitchen. "No, honey, the pantry is all done. Mommy will give you some food."

I put the "First and Then" sign on the table with a picture of a chicken nugget after "First" and a fish cracker after "Then."

He walked away.

The bus came and took a hungry Zack to school.

He came home later that day with a note in his backpack. It read, "Zack didn't eat today."

OUR HEARTS BROKE. ZACK LOOKED AT US LIKE WE WERE TRAITORS. WE HELD OUR SHAKY GROUND.

At dinner I again put out the sign and pictures. Zack cried. Jay and I grimaced. We couldn't give in now or he would never eat the way we wanted him to, but tears were his best weapon. Our hearts broke. Zack looked at us like we were traitors. We held our shaky ground.

The next morning we went through the same routine.

He didn't eat again. The note came home from school saying Zack had eaten one bite of nugget for snack and two bites for lunch.

He refused to eat dinner and cried himself to sleep. I almost broke, but held on.

On the third day Zack wouldn't eat breakfast or snack, but he ate one bite of peanut butter and jelly sandwich and three chicken nuggets for lunch, rewarded bite for bite with Pringles, Cheetos, and apple juice. He had three more nuggets for dinner with fish crackers, milk, and applesauce, making it the most well-rounded meal he'd ever consumed.

We continued on, but Zack only ate when he was too hungry to refuse. We had to give up the chicken nuggets because he just couldn't seem to make himself eat them without gagging, but within a week he was eating peanut butter and jelly sandwiches, homemade carrot bread, and applesauce. It was a major breakthrough.

"He's sitting at the table with us!" I mouthed with glee over Zack's head to Jay at the end of our kitchen table. We were ecstatic at the change in our dinner hour. All four of us around the table at last!

"It was worth the stress," Jay said with a smile, as he looked at Zack sitting quietly in his place, eating a peanut butter and jelly sandwich. Sure, he wasn't eating our food yet, but a PB & J was health food for Zack.

Overall, Zack's eating is healthier, but only because we deny access to what he considers to be the good stuff until he's eaten what we put in front of him. The struggle goes on. Still, for him and for us, the improvements in Zack's diet and eating together as a family more often, as well as all the growth that took strenuous discipline on everyone's part, have been huge achievements worth celebration.

"Perseverance is not a long race; it is many short races one after another."

—WALTER ELLIOTT

Discipline your son and he will give you peace; he will bring delight to your soul.

—PROVERBS 29:17

Chapter Thirteen

WHEN DID LIFE
GET TO BE SO GOOD?

When Zack was three, I was told that when a child with special needs reaches the age of seven, the miracle workers go home. At seven and a half, the official "golden opportunity" of early childhood intervention is over, but it's now that we are reaping the most benefit from those early years of therapy. They formed the foundation that Zack is building upon now to master skills we only hoped he would acquire. In fact, this is the first year that a speech therapist has told me she believes he will grow to be quite verbal. I took that comment to the bank and deposited it! And this year's school Individual Education Plan meeting was the most positive I have ever experienced. Zack progressed by over a year in every category of development except one.

Another much-applauded development for Zack this year is his increased desire to socialize with peers. Because of this, he has begun to go into a typical classroom each day for lunchtime. We weren't sure he was enjoying himself there until one day when his teacher kept him with his special-education class.

Toward the end of their lunchtime, Zack signed, "bathroom." When he was allowed to go, he took his lunchsack and high-tailed it to the other end of the school building to join his new group of friends for lunch!

This short time of mainstreaming has not only been good for Zack, it has also blessed the typically developing children he joins for lunch. One little girl was concerned when he first joined their classroom because she has an aunt with Downs Syndrome around whom she is nervous. After a few weeks with Zack sitting next to her at lunch, she reported to her mother that Zack is adorable and has his own secret language, which she finds very intriguing. Her mother told me that they have a family gathering coming up soon and that the little girl feels like she wants to get to know the aunt whom she previously feared.

WHILE MY DREAMS FOR A "NORMAL" FAMILY HAVEN'T COME TRUE, OTHER DREAMS HAVE.

Along with increased development, every month seems to bring a miracle of deeper connection with us. Over time, as Zack began to join briefly in our family activities, our sadness over his isolation eased. For this to happen, we had to learn to let Zack do it his way. So he wanders in and out of our social interactions, retreating to his room and music or outside to our yard when he needs to. This makes connecting with us possible for Zack, without adding to the stress of his social anxiety.

A treasured breakthrough occurred this Christmas, when Zack gave us the gift of playing a board game with our family. It was after dinner that we set up Sorry on our kitchen table. Zack stayed nearby, so I gave him the yellow pawns to play with, hoping he would allow me to move them around the board like the rest of us were doing. I had tried this a few months before, but he had refused to let them leave their "Start" circle.

I debated pushing him to be more involved in the game tonight, but I finally decided to try it again. So, when Zack turned over a two, I said, "Zack, you get to move out of 'Start'!" and moved his piece. Surprising us all, he didn't object. As the game progressed, he let me move each of his pieces around the board, and he even counted with me some of the time.

I WONDER WHEN MY LIFE WENT FROM BEING SO HARD TO BEING SO GOOD.

Forty-five minutes later we were still playing, and Zack won! As I watched him spinning on the floor, I thought about the "normal" family I had planned. I realized that normally Taylor wouldn't have cheered when his younger brother beat him at a board game. Normally I wouldn't see my capable elder son growing in kindness as he interacts with his brother. Normally we wouldn't celebrate just because Zack was joining us in an activity. And normally we wouldn't see the small steps of development we witness in Zack as miracles.

While my dreams for a "normal" family haven't come true, other dreams have, some with fanfare, some quietly.

Today I've spent hours in my garden, attacking dandelions with my shovel. Zack wanders around me as I work. He pulls on plants and looks at flowers, just like I'm doing. All the while, he is repeating, "Yay," in a deep, gravelly voice.

"Yes, Zack, it is a yay kind of day, isn't it?" I say. He chuckles in agreement. The clouds make it hazy, but it's warm enough to make us sweat, and the promise of summer is in the air. I look up at my boy as he comes over to pat my back enthusiastically, leaning against me for a few moments.

As I pause with my boy pressed against me, I wonder when my life went from being so hard to being so good.

MY FEARS DROPPED AWAY AS EACH ONE WAS PROVEN FALSE.

It's been five and a half years since Zack's diagnosis, and somewhere in that time my fears dropped away as each one was proven false: Zack and I bonded; our family is happy and close; Zack got potty-trained; we have respite workers and teachers to help us; Zack continues to progress; oh, and yes, I love him more than ever. He may never talk fluently, at least in a language we understand, or live on his own, but he has a pleasant disposition and easily wiggles his way into people's hearts.

I still remember how it felt the first time Zack held my hand. He was five years old before he would uncurl his tight little fist and take my hand when we crossed the street. Before that I had to hold on to his arm to keep him by my side. I thought it would always be that way, having long since given up the dream of those tiny toddler fingers wrapped around one or two of my own.

It's such a common thing, to hold your child's hand. Not something a mom gives much thought to, unless her child refuses to do it. Then it becomes a focal point of every venture outside the safe walls of home and fenced yard. I yearned for that little hand to hold mine. I longed for what it signified— that he was mine and I was his. I didn't want to hold his shirt like a woman holds her purse or her pet; I wanted to hold his hand!

Then one day, as I grabbed for Zack's fist, a miracle happened. It opened up. Palm to palm, his little fingers curled around mine; our hands fit perfectly. His untouched palm was softer than silk. Two and a half years later my heart still does a little skip whenever I feel his palm against mine.

Now Zack comes and pulls me into his play many times a day. I look down at my son's bright face and hear his sweet laughter bubbling over as I acquiesce to leaving my world and entering his.

My boy's shining sea-foam eyes hold a glimpse of what is true. The truth is that Zack doesn't live in my world. He floats between it and his own—a world where numbers and scales of development don't mean a thing, where repetition and predictability are essential, and where the most important parts of the day are music, being tickled, and playing peekaboo. In Zack's world all that counts is loving and being loved.

SOMEHOW, SOMEWHERE ALONG THE LINE, THIS "TRAGEDY" IN MY LIFE HAS TURNED INTO A MIRACLE.

Maybe seeing the value in Zack's world and learning to relax in it gave me the key to accepting it. Or maybe it was learning to connect on his terms, for there is no doubt that the bond I longed for with him is strongly forged. No, we will never, this side of heaven, do many of the things that I enjoy doing with Taylor, but Zack and I are professionals at peekaboo!

Albert Einstein said, "There are two ways to live your life. One is as though nothing is a miracle. The other is as though everything is a miracle." Somehow, somewhere along the line, this "tragedy" in my life has turned into a miracle. It is a miracle of grace that I wouldn't have recognized without Zack. Grace, not just for what is ahead but also for the nitty-gritty details of the here and now. The depth of my grief has been matched by surprising heights of joy and wonder. For that I am very grateful.

⬿ *Happiness cannot be traveled to, owned, earned, worn, or consumed. Happiness is the spiritual experience of living every minute with love, grace, and gratitude.*

—DENIS WAITLEY

⬿ *And we know that in all things God works for the good of those who love him, who have been called according to his purpose.*

—ROMANS 8:28

⬿ LAZY SUMMER DAYS

> *Your small palm warms my face*
> *with welcome caresses,*
> *treasured affection worth*
> *years of waiting.*
> *We swing,*
> *cradled in a hammock,*
> *transported by calypso music*
> *to our private world.*
> *Little boy fingers*
> *reach up*
> *to wrap Mommy's curls*
> *round and round.*
> *Your eyes sparkle*
> *like the shallow water*
> *off a distant island's*
> *bleached sand beach.*
> *Your body calm*
> *in my arms,*
> *we float on a sea*
> *of peaceful connection.*

—ELIZABETH GRIFFIN

Resources

www.disabilityinfo.gov—A comprehensive federal Web site designed to serve people with disabilities.

Office of Special Education Programs
U. S. Department of Education
330 C Street, SW Room #3080
Washington, D.C. 20202-2570
(202) 205-8828

www.thearc.org—The ARC of the United States (Advocates for the Rights of Citizens with Developmental Disabilities). This organization has many helpful programs, including a Parent to Parent support program. (301) 565-3842

www.autism-resources.com—Frequently asked questions, links

www.autism-society.org—Autism Society of America

www.feat.org—Families for Early Autism Treatment

www.fragilex.org—National Fragile X Foundation. This is a wonderful resource of information, support, and community for families and people affected by fragile X syndrome. (800) 688-8765

www.fraxa.org—FRAXA Research Foundation. This organization researches treatment and cures for fragile X syndrome. (978) 462-1866

ENDNOTES

Chapter 1

1. Henri J. M. Nouwen. *Life of the Beloved* (New York: Crossroad, 1995), pp. 48–49.

Chapter 3

1. Sheila Walsh. *Gifts for Your Soul* (Grand Rapids, Mich.: Zondervan), 1997.

Chapter 5

1. George Eliot (Mary Ann Evans) quoted in Helen Gouldner and Mary Symons Strong in *Speaking of Friendship: Middle-Class Women and Their Friends* (New York: Greenwood Press, 1987), p. 7.

Chapter 7

1. William Barclay. *The Gospel of John*, vol. 2, rev. ed. (Philadelphia: Westminster Press, 1975), p. 180.

Chapter 8

1. Jan Dravecky. *Hope for a Woman's Soul: Meditations to Energize Your Spirit* (Grand Rapids, Mich.: Zondervan, 2000), p. 161.

Chapter 9

1. Viktor E. Frankl. *Man's Search for Meaning* (New York: Washington Square Press, 1997), p. 64.
2. Mother Teresa. *Words to Love By* (Notre Dame, Ind.: Ave Maria Press, 1983), p. 68.
3. Martha Washington, written in a letter to her friend Mercy Otis Warren, while First Lady of the United States, c. 1789.